Simple Steps

Simple Steps

Ten Things You Can Do to Create an Exceptional Life

Dr. Arthur Caliandro
with Barry Lenson

McGRAW-HILL

New York   San Francisco   Washington, D.C.   Auckland   Bogotá
Caracas   Lisbon   London   Madrid   Mexico City   Milan
Montreal   New Delhi   San Juan   Singapore
Sydney   Tokyo   Toronto

Library of Congress Catalog Card Number: 99-074661

McGraw-Hill

A Division of The **McGraw-Hill** Companies

Copyright © 2000 by The McGraw-Hill Companies, Inc. All rights reserved. Printed in the United States of America. Except as permitted under the United States Copyright Act of 1976, no part of this publication may be reproduced or distributed in any form or by any means, or stored in a database or retrieval system, without the prior written permission of the publisher.

1 2 3 4 5 6 7 8 9 0   DOC/DOC   9 0 9 8 7 6 5 4 3 2 1 0 9

ISBN 0-07-134797-6

This book was set in Minion by MM Design 2000, Inc.
Printed and bound by R. R. Donnelley & Sons Company.

McGraw-Hill books are available at special quantity discounts to use as premiums and sales promotions, or for use in corporate training programs. For more information, please write to the Director of Special Sales, McGraw-Hill, 11 West 19th Street, New York, NY 10011.
Or contact your local bookstore.

This book is printed on recycled, acid-free paper
containing a minimum of 50% recycled, de-inked fiber.

To my sons,
Paul and Charles

Contents

Author's Note

When I encounter a book like this, I first read it for what the author has to say. I underline sections in red and often write in the margin words and phrases that seem relevant for me. In this way, I can later open the book and, at a glance, read again the words and ideas that seemed most helpful and poignant to me.

This process affords me the chance of absorbing the wisdom of the ideas. Over time, the thoughts that meant the most to me may become part of my consciousness. They eventually may become me—or perhaps I will become them.

Just reading a book like this quickly, and once, won't be helpful. If that is what you do, the best that can happen is that you will get a general sense of what the author believes. I hope you will do more than that with *Simple Steps.* I hope you will make this book your friend.

In time, as you live with the ideas this book contains—of kindness, quiet, forgiveness, and the rest—they will become your new reality—and you will become a new person.

Introduction

Would you like to enjoy an exceptional, fulfilling life?

I think most people would answer yes to that question.

I often recall a story told by a college professor about one of his former students. On the first night that young man was on campus at a welcoming reception at the professor's house, he suddenly blurted out, "I'm going to make my life a miracle."

And he went on to do well in his life and career.

I am drawn to the spirit of that young man. He wanted to live an exceptional life. He wanted his life to be special.

I believe living such a life is possible for anyone who chooses to do so, regardless of circumstances or age.

Yet doing so is not easy for anyone. In his books, the author Scott Peck accurately describes life as both difficult and complex—an enormous challenge. Or, as summarized in my favorite definition of life:

Life is a series of problem-solving situations.

The success or failure of our lives depends on how effectively we meet and solve whatever problems lie before us. And those problems can be quite complex. As some wise person once said, there are no simple problems after kindergarten.

We can be given charts and procedures, systems and formulas, for making our lives better. Yet complex answers seldom solve complex problems. We can best deal with the process of change by taking simple steps, one at a time, and doing so with thoughtfulness and patience.

I have learned that each change in life, each part of one's journey, starts with movement in the heart and mind. Real change comes from deep within, and it comes in one's own time.

Some of the wisest advice I ever heard was given to me at a New Year's gathering one year. I was in a small group of people, and we were discussing resolutions for coming year. A man in my group suggested to me that success is most likely when we make just one resolution, focus on it alone, and then patiently give it plenty of time.

That advice has worked for me on many occasions—from my resolve to lose weight to the more difficult challenge of forgiving someone who had hurt me. Yet in all cases, a singular focus and a patient heart can make miracles happen.

Your life can dramatically change for the better when you make the decision to take simple decisive steps like these, one at a time.

Decide to adopt a positive attitude.
Resolve to be kind in all circumstances.
Refuse to give up despite all obstacles.
Leave the past behind and move on.

Steps like these can ultimately change your life for the better. We'll explore them—and more—in the pages that follow.

Elation, empowerment, and excitement about life can begin today. It can surely happen, in the thoughts and insights we are about to share together in this joyous little book.

Simple Steps

CHAPTER ONE

Your Attitude Is Your Future

A ttitude stands as the one area of your life where you are in complete and total control.

External events can change what you do with your life, how long you live, where you live, and other factors. Other people can force you to accept their routines or ideas.

Attitude is different. No one can make you accept an attitude you don't want.

Each of us has the power to choose a positive attitude, or a negative one. Of all the Simple Steps we'll explore together in this book, I put this one first. It is the bedrock beneath all the other steps that follow.

Your attitude is your future, pure and simple. Choosing the right one will profoundly change your life at once, today.

Decide on Your Attitude

In May 1985, the Dutch Consulate asked my church to sponsor a Sunday service commemorating the fortieth anniversary of the liberation of Holland. It was an inspiring day. Volunteers hung banners in the church, the choir sang special music, and many dignitaries attended. Among them were the American pilots who had dropped food into occupied Holland—and the farmers who had received that food.

For these people to meet face to face was extraordinarily emotional and meaningful. There were tears and embraces. For depth of emotion, I can't recall too many occasions to compare with it.

After the service, a commemorative luncheon was held, where I had the opportunity to be seated at a table with several people who were new to me. Among them was a woman of about sixty. She was a very lovely, elegant person— pleasant, warm, and gentle. Yet, from the lines in her face, I sensed that her life had been interesting and challenging.

As we began to talk, her story unfolded. She told me that she had been sent to a German concentration camp when she was a teenager. While there, she saw the smoke come from the chineys of the gas ovens. That smoke represented the bodies of every member of her family, since she alone had survived.

She described the scene to me when the day of liberation finally came and she walked into freedom, owning nothing more than the clothing she was wearing. She told me that, at that moment, she did something that would affect the rest of her life.

"I had a decision to make. My life was ahead of me. I could decide to live a happy life, or an unhappy one, full of resentment and hatred. I decided I would be happy."

She went on, "It hasn't been easy. Not one day or night has gone by when I haven't either had a nightmare or some harrowing memory of those four years. But I have had a very good life. I am a happy woman."

No one looking into this woman's eyes would ever accuse her of being superficial, a Pollyanna—someone who chose to see only artificially positive aspects of life, while shutting out all knowledge of the negatives. She was a realist who chose to be positive. And that is something to aspire to.

She knew, even in the darkest of days, that her attitude was the factor that would determine whether her life would sink down into misery or rise up into fulfillment. She saw that her attitude was her future. And that the choice was hers alone.

Each of us, regardless of circumstances, has that power.

Take that step. It's the first—and possibly the most profound—of the many we'll share together in this book.

Put Some Oil on
Your Hinges

A few years ago, due to road construction, my usual forty-five-minute commute was doubled. I was spending between ninety minutes and two hours in my car, twice a day! It was horrendous.

During this time, my wife was away, traveling on business. Each night we would check in by phone, and I was quick to whine and complain about the frustrations of my commute. Poor me!

She was the first to tell me I was suffering from a bad attitude. And even after she told me, it took me a while to see she was right.

It is easy to see another person's bad attitude but difficult to admit our own.

I should have realized that my negative attitude was really getting to me. I wasn't sleeping well at night. I felt nervous. I also recalled the devastating effects that stress and tension had exerted on my health in years past, resulting in major illnesses. Every person's body, after all, has points of vulnerability that are prone to weakness or failure when the individual is subjected to continued stress. And the early signs of such problems were already beginning to show.

Yet thanks to my wife, I began to get myself in tow. I began working to relax in the car. I allowed myself more travel time and tried not to let the traffic and the slow movement get to me. I worked to get back in charge of myself. While I couldn't change the traffic flow, I could change my attitude toward it.

Had I not changed, my bad outlook could have exerted a negative force on my health—and by extension, a negative effect on my wife and all the other people around me.

As I sometimes say when I give a talk on the topic of attitude,

Big doors swing on little hinges.

I find this a wonderful thought. Most of the time, we don't see the hinges on a door. We don't pay attention to them. They're small and hidden, yet without them, the door would not function at all.

Our attitudes, too, are the little hinges on which the big doors of our lives swing. The wrong attitude brings wear and tear, finally tearing the door down.

We can't control life's negative circumstances—the doubled commutes, long lines at the grocery, aches and pains, or late-night calls from marketers. Those are life's invariables. Yet we can do something to cope with them. We can control how we relate to them.

It's a simple choice, a simple step you can take. The right attitude will keep all the mechanisms of your life in top working order.

Stop Justifying
a Negative Outlook

I recently met with the mother of a young man who had become morose, withdrawn, surly, and unambitious. He was all that, despite the fact that he enjoyed a good family, a secure home, economic security, and many remarkable advantages. His parents had read books, sent him to prestigious schools, and taken him for evaluation and counseling by prominent psychotherapists.

"What are we going to do? What should we try now?" his mother asked me. As much as I wanted to produce some magic wand for her, I could only answer, "Your son will get better when he decides to get better. You can provide a good, caring context for him to change. But ultimately, it's a choice only he can make for himself."

It often puzzles me to see people with material security, friends, freedoms, and good means who indulge themselves with bad attitudes. They have problems, yes, as does every human being, yet they are bogged down with negative attitudes.

On the other hand, there are some people who live in circumstances that might justify bad attitudes. They live with illness, poverty, bereavement, and other cataclysmic problems, yet they have terrific attitudes.

If it is possible to simply choose a good attitude, why do some people resolutely go the other way, preferring to become mired in negativism, bad expectations, even despair?

We can psychologize, psychoanalyze, and rationalize why a person has the right to have a negative attitude:

- *An unhappy childhood*

- *Parents who were aloof and uncaring*

- *A period of ill health*

- *A marriage in turmoil*

Yet, to my mind, none of those excuses really justifies a bad attitude since a bad attitude never makes things better.

The self-justifying causes people mention for negativity are relatively unimportant. They serve only to justify the reactive person's need to slip into that well-worn, bad attitude for another day.

This is taking a reactive approach to life. It implies that we have no control over our lives—that we are powerless pawns, totally controlled by other people or forces beyond our control.

A good attitude can be chosen in circumstances that are as close to hell as any we might find on earth. A bad attitude can arise in circumstances that are full of love and advantages.

It is a personal decision that you can make from wherever you are.

Take the Higher Road

"Take the higher road." Those are words you will read again in later chapters of this book. Simple as they may sound, they lie at the center of many of the daily choices we make as we determine the trajectory of our lives —the path we will take.

Those words also lie at the crux of attitude.

The truth is that we are all offered many opportunities each day to assume a bad attitude toward our surroundings, in many small ways:

— Your colleagues at work are engaging in a gripe session about the people who run your company. Will you join the complaining, or will you direct a positive attitude at the problems they are "acting out upon" with negativism?

— Or perhaps the other parents of your child's classmates are directing a stream of complaints at the school your children attend together. If there is a basis to their complaints, you can either go down into negativism or raise the level of the discussion to the positives and what could be done to make things better.

In other words, you can take the higher road, which leads to better outcomes and better results.

Which way should *you* go?

It is important to become attuned to making those decisions, that each of us is called upon to make many times through the course of a day.

Few decisions will influence the quality of our lives as much as these.

Test Drive
Your New Attitude Today

I recall one woman in a church where I previously served. She was a committed member of our spiritual community and a woman of strong faith. Yet she had a palpably negative outlook on life. When she was part of a committee, other members silently dreaded going into meetings with her. I certainly did!

Her heart may have been good, but she seemed to filter the world through a screen of negativism. Everyone, in her view, was trying to take advantage of her, marginalize her, dismiss her opinions and ideas. She was abrasive, combative, and obstructive.

Finally, at one meeting, a young man had simply had enough and told her that her negative attitude was making the group's work much more difficult than it really needed to be. The rest of us in the room were stunned into silence since we had just heard the very words that had been playing through most of our minds. We waited to see what kind of blow-up would ensue.

The woman was completely surprised by the accusation that she had a negative attitude. She simply had no notion that she was perceived so negatively by the people around her. Her negative attitude was invisible to her.

A surprise? Not really. Negative attitudes are like that. As one sage once said, we are not given the power to see ourselves as other people do. It is very easy to notice other people's bad outlooks and very difficult to perceive our own.

I often tell a story about two young men who were hired to run the customer-service department in a department store. In other words, the *complaint* department. Now, these young men were fresh out of school. The store didn't give them much training, but essentially threw them onto the "front lines" to deal with irate customers as best they could. They were bright and personable and certainly able to do a good job.

Yet these young fellows didn't handle the job at all well. In fact, they acted like hotshots and adopted an "eye-for-an-eye" attitude regarding customers. Essentially, they slipped into a mood of responding in kind, meeting hostility with hostility, indifference with indifference, defensiveness with defensiveness. They were completely reactive, letting the customers determine how they would respond.

Soon the job started getting to them. One night after work, they went out to a bar to almost literally cry in their beer. As they discussed their frustrations about the job and the difficulties of dealing with unhappy people, one of them noticed a sign over the bartender's head. He said to his friend, "Look at that sign. We've tried everything else, but not what that slogan says!"

Be kind. Everybody is fighting a tough battle.

They changed their thinking almost immediately. And they set a new strategy. They would try to be kind to customers and strive to anticipate their needs, truly work to serve them. After a few days of trying to do things the new way, one of them said to the other, "Have you noticed? We have a different kind of person coming into the department. People are a lot nicer."

That's a lighthearted story—one I often embellish in the telling. The point is that they created an atmosphere around themselves that affected the people coming in. And the whole situation improved. But this story also contains a deeper message about the force of attitude.

Choosing a good attitude is like casting those many loaves upon the waters of your life. The benefits that come back to you are usually unpredictable, unexpected—and deeply enriching to your life.

Remember the Toll Taker

If you ever drive on the New Jersey Turnpike, at Exit 16 you just might be fortunate enough to find my favorite toll collector. He's the one who always says, "Good morning! How are you? What a great day!"

Since he must say those words five thousand times a day, consider the cumulative, positive effect this man is having on the lives of other people.

A few weeks ago, I flew into Newark Airport. I got into a cab and struck up a conversation with the driver. I asked whether he knew my favorite toll collector.

"Oh, yeah, that guy!" the driver answered. "He's the nicest toll collector anywhere! But have you found the one at the Holland Tunnel yet? There's one there who is just as good. Sometimes cars line up to get to him. People would rather wait an extra minute to get him than go to someone else."

I didn't know there was a friendly toll collector at the Holland Tunnel, too. But the next time I'm headed that way, I'm going to look for him.

The moment you enter the space occupied by a kind person with a strongly positive attitude, you have a wonderful power directed at you. You feel positive, elevated, inspired. Suddenly, new things are possible for you.

Would you not like to have that kind of impact on the lives of countless other people? Would you not like them to come looking for you when they need a little uplift, a little inspiration?

Wouldn't we all? And we can, with attitude. The choice is up to us.

Stop Justifying

"Yes, I may have a bad attitude. But I have good reasons, and I am justified in having it."

We've all heard those words, or spoken them ourselves.

I've seen that attitude emerge frequently—often, when I've been counseling men and women whose marriages are troubled. In such circumstances, there is often a lot of blame involved. People say, "I know I was part of the problem. I made mistakes. I may have been wrong much of the time, *but. . .*"

And that *but* serves as the trigger for self-justifying explanations of why this person has the right to feel hurt and vindictive toward the spouse. I regularly say, "Is it possible for you to separate yourself from all the negatives, and just look at yourself? Get a sense of yourself and what your responsibility to yourself is?"

That's asking a lot, asking a person to get away from dwelling on all the perceived unfairness—To take a good attitude and be truly defenseless.

In my many years of ministering to a large, vibrant congregation of people, I have seen more instances than I can recall where seemingly insurmountable obstacles could be moved out of the way with the right attitude, with the result that a person's life could indeed move forward.

I have seen terminally ill people become well. I have seen marriages saved. I have seen troubled families knitted closer together. There have been dramatic breakthroughs in careers.

I have seen attitude changes cause books to be written, music to be performed, and lives to be transformed in more ways than I have space here to report.

A good attitude costs nothing. It's a small investment. Having a good one takes no more time than having a bad one. And it all starts like a little kernel, a small choice that you make calmly and quietly within you, like a wonderful little surprise gift you decide you will deliver to the waiting world.

It is a small choice, but it promises big results. Why not make that choice right now, even before you turn this page and start the next chapter? The power resides only in you.

CHAPTER TWO

Tap Your Inner Momentum

O NE of the worst things that can happen to any of us in life is that we become what I call "quick quitters."

Sometimes, as soon as we are confronted by a major problem, we run away from it. Pessimism and a lack of self-belief cause us to take the easier course, and we simply stop trying. Or, faced with a setback, we try something else, declare the troubling problem "off limits" without even thinking of trying again.

This kind of thinking permeates many lives—most often, the lives of people who are unhappy and unfulfilled. Yet there is a better way.

We can tap our inner momentum. When faced with a setback or even outright failure, we can keep moving and try again.

Admittedly, keeping hope alive and refusing to be stopped does not always lead on to victory. However, refusing to be a quick quitter is one of the surest ways I know to shift the odds of success heavily in your favor.

As Sir Winston Churchill said to his fellow English citizens just when England was at its greatest danger in World War II, "Gentlemen, the situation is grave, but I find it rather inspiring."

Or, as the physician Dr. Bernie Siegel says to patients who have a disease from which no one has recovered, "Would you like to be the first?"

Both these people knew that, even though some obstacles seem insurmountable, success hinges on the ability to keep on hoping and striving for victory.

We're talking about miracles here. But miracles do happen. Most often, they happen to people who realize they can exercise the choice to refuse to be stopped.

Keep Moving Ahead

I'd like to share a special story with you—one that occupies a special place in my heart because I once told it in a sermon, and Dr. Norman Vincent Peale heard it and paid me a high compliment, saying it was a powerful illustration.

"Arthur, that is one of your best," he said, "one of your very best." A very high compliment, indeed.

With that said, let me share the story with you.

Many years ago, when my sons Paul and Chuck were little, I went camping with my family in the Grand Teton National Park in Wyoming. Our camp was located in a little area called Leigh Lake—surely one of the most beautiful spots I have ever seen. Trees were everywhere around this little lake, and the view looked as it must have ten thousand years ago, virtually untouched by human beings. Across the lake were the snow-covered peaks of Mount St. John and Mount Moran. Above them all towered the Grand Teton, a hundred feet higher than even the famed Jungfrau in Switzerland. It was absolutely awe inspiring.

Now, as you'd expect, my attention was often directed toward those high, majestic peaks, and I found them deeply inspiring. Yet one morning, I found some inspiration in a very different, and far lower, place.

On that morning, I was by the lake, where the only other life forms I found were some birds, a chipmunk, and a few other campers who, like me, were early risers.

But then as I looked down at my feet, I saw a solitary black ant.

That little insect walked in front of my foot, with its little legs moving along in a quick, easy rhythm. I realized I had never really watched an ant before, but I recalled that the Bible mentions them several times, attributing to them such traits as wisdom and resourcefulness.

I thought it might be interesting to test this little creature's resourcefulness. So I made a little hill out of sand in his path to see how he would get around it. It must have seemed like a mountain to him. Yet up it he walked, without breaking stride, and he went right down the other side.

Next, I dug a little hole to create a valley across his path. He went right in, then out, without stopping. Next, I put a good-sized stone in his path. He tried to climb it, struggled a bit, fell back. Then he seemed to reconsider the situation, and he walked around it.

Finally, I tried one last obstacle. I put a little stick in front of him. He struggled with that problem, too, until he found a way around the obstacle by shifting direction and seeking an alternate route.

That little ant had passed some pretty tough tests. Yet during all of them, what did he do? He kept moving. At no time—not even for an instant—did he stop. As far as I could tell, he never changed the fundamental activity he was engaged in, which was moving ahead. What momentum! I thought, too, that he did not complain. Unlike a human being who is confronted by obstacles, he didn't go to a friend to complain. He didn't give in to fatigue and take a breather. He did not sit there and think about his problems before trying again. He didn't go back to the ant colony to think things over or come back with a committee from his ant government.

He knew there was only one thing to do—to keep on going. He seemed to know that was all he needed to eventually arrive at his destination. And I suppose that, once I stopped putting obstacles in his path, he eventually got where he was going.

Curious, isn't it, that this lesson should come to me not from the heights, but from somewhere nearer the ground—right at my very feet?

Yet it was, for me, a vivid demonstration of a vital message.

We don't have to be stopped by every obstacle that life puts in our paths. As thinking beings, we might need to pause and reflect, to consider our options and make plans. But at the most fundamental level, success hinges on our ability to tap into our natural, wonderful momentum. Like that little ant, we can refuse to be stopped. We can keep going, and we can learn as we go.

People who patiently persist finally see their dreams come true. For them, persistence makes all the difference.

Don't Let Setbacks
Stall You

One night in December 1914, Thomas Edison's laboratories went up in flames, and virtually everything that he had been working on was burning up. His son Charles, who was twenty-four at the time, was looking everywhere for his father in the crowd, feeling very concerned. After all, his father was sixty-seven years old, and getting older, and his life's work was going up in smoke before his eyes.

When Charles found his father, he was astonished to see that his father's face was nearly radiant. "Charles, Charles, where is your mother?" he said. "Go find her. She'll never see anything like this again."

Later, as Thomas Edison was walking around the ruins, he said, "Isn't it wonderful that all of your mistakes can be burned up?"

Three weeks later, he produced his first prototype of a phonograph and went on to experiment and invent for nearly another two decades, until he was well into his eighties.

Edison was an exceptional man. Yet, as we know from his own writings, he was not an exceptional youth. In fact, he admits that in his younger years, he was full of self-doubts, reinforced by the feedback he was getting from other people. They saw few exceptional abilities in him—certainly, nothing that would indicate that his life would be filled with so many extraordinary achievements.

Could it be that his progress, and his successes, hinged on his ability to keep moving ahead, through obstacles?

Certainly we know his now-famous quotes on how he achieved some of his successes:

After creating hundreds of non-working light bulbs, he is said to have observed, "Now I know hundreds of reasons why a light bulb will not work." And what may be his most famous observation, he stated that "Genius is one percent inspiration and ninety-nine percent perspiration."

Those are well-known quotes, to be sure. But they convey an important message to all of us.

The success we achieve doesn't always hinge on great talent or intelligence. It hinges, more often than not, on one simple decision.

The decision to keep on going.

Keep Your Goals Flexible

There's another lesson we can learn, too, from that resourceful little ant I mentioned at the start of this chapter. That lesson is to keep your goals flexible.

When that ant encountered something he was incapable of climbing over, he didn't just keep walking straight into it again and again, hitting his head, without changing direction. He shifted course, found another way around—and kept his journey on track.

There is a lesson to be learned in that, about the way we set our life goals and pursue them. I've noticed that people who accomplish a great deal know better than to keep hitting their heads against the same high obstacles. They know that life's goals are adaptable. They can change.

Positive change is not always comfortable. More often than not, it requires breaks in routines and familiar ways. Here are some statements I've heard from people who have encountered obstacles in their path—and who are finding their way around:

> *I've been out of work for nearly a year. Even when I think I've found a job that I could handle quite capably, I just don't get excited about it—and that lack of enthusiasm shows when I go in to interview. I think it's time for something new.*

> *I thought I wanted to work in the legal profession, but I'm finding myself called to do something different with my life.*

My parents always wanted me to excel as a classical pianist, and I tried. I think I'm destined to find my happiness in another kind of work—although it might disappoint them.

Obstacles come in many shapes and sizes—and they can suddenly appear in many places in our lives. In most cases, they are really valuable signs that our goals and ambitions are not serving us as well as they once did.

More and more today, I encounter people who are empowering themselves to make midcareer changes and transformations—often involving considerable risk and sacrifice. The growth they achieve is usually greater than they could have realized by remaining stuck in repetitive patterns—another name for "ruts"— that were no longer moving their lives forward.

I know one woman, for instance, who enjoyed a successful career as an executive for several decades, but who then became a teacher. She describes this change as her "new lease on life." And I know a man who went the other way. He left the teaching profession and became an executive at an advertising agency. He, too, is elated at his life change.

As Oliver Wendell Holmes wrote, "One thing I've found out about this life is this. It's not so much where we stand, but in what direction we're moving."

What a profound, yet simple thought.

Embrace change. When we do, and the change is the right one, it's like having the wind at our backs, filling us with strong energy. We can move our lives ahead again with confidence, and our lives become renewed and refreshed.

Learn to Relish Life's Challenges

Problems are natural. In fact, on the day you have no problems, you have arrived at a dead end in your life because you are not being challenged to grow.

As one of my favorite professors often would say, life is a series of problem-solving situations.

I believe that the words we use to describe challenges can make a tremendous difference in our ability to move past them. I find it immensely helpful to substitute the energizing word "challenge" for the negative word "problem." When we get in the habit of saying, "I have to face this challenge," we enhance our ability to grow. And when we say, "I have this problem," we lose the energy to get the hard work done.

The nature of the human experience, after all, is to overcome. We see it reflected in many places, including these inspiring words from the Twenty-Third Psalm:

I will walk through the valley of the shadow of death.

It does not say we shall *dwell* in that valley. We are only moving through.

Learning to view life's daily tests as challenges is one of the surest ways to emerge from that valley into a far better and brighter place.

Don't Worry, Do Something

Worry is one of the greatest momentum blockers I know of. Worriers, possibly more than anyone else, remain immobilized by fear. They're stuck.

Yet what is worry, really? An enemy made up of subterfuge and mist. It is a series of "what ifs" that immobilize the worried into a state of nonaction.

Yet when we confront worry, it vanishes and frees us to move ahead. How can we give up worrying?

One effective approach can be found in a simple two-word formula. I'd encourage you to hold it in the center of your mind until it becomes second nature to you. When a situation arises that would normally cause you to worry, coach yourself to think.

Do something!

In other words, "Take action." When we take action—the earlier the better—we nip worry in the bud.

Consider stories from Scripture. We know that people often went to Jesus with their problems—often, problems of health or disease. And Jesus always did something to help.

Now, after Jesus healed someone, he usually dismissed that person with the words, "Go in peace. *Your faith has made you well.*"

In other words, the person had empowered him- or herself to get around the problem.

This lesson underscores the reality that the ultimate responsibility for moving ahead is ours. Other people may move obstacles out of our way, but we are the prime motivators for our own progress.

Now, you might respond to this concept by saying that there are times when you simply cannot do something. And, of course, that is sometimes true. Circumstances really can be beyond our control at times. Perhaps we are waiting for someone else to make a decision before we can act, or we have to delay while we are saving money or otherwise put our plans on hold. Or we are working our way through a problem, and it is just going to take a little time before it will be resolved.

But even in such situations as these there is something you can do. You can completely devote yourself to the problem. You can hold it up to a higher power. You can pray about it. You can approach it from a *spiritual* perspective as well as from a *worldly* one.

As a very wise person once said to me, "Why worry when you can pray?"

This thought can bring calm. It can relieve anxiety. It can help us look at things more clearly because it brings a "higher" overview of the problem that is holding us back.

So, the two steps I've found that really let us move ahead despite worry are

> *First, do something.*
>
> *Second, hold the immobilizing worry up before a higher power.*

This two-part strategy embodies a wonderful internal balance—a balance that's made up of action and contemplation. In my experience, it's a combination that works.

Help Someone Else

When you help other people overcome their obstacles, you also find a way to help yourself get around your own.

A number of years ago, we started an "I Have a Dream Program" at Marble Collegiate Church, dedicated to helping disadvantaged inner-city children. It's one of the most ambitious programs ever to emerge from our church.

We started by adopting an entire class of students at an elementary school in Harlem, committing ourselves to assisting them to prepare for college. We envisioned that when participants finished high school and qualified for college, we would guarantee their college education.

It was a challenging undertaking. We had high hopes at the beginning, then somewhat reduced expectations as years went by, and many kids either dropped out or didn't perform up to their abilities. Some of the kids came from backgrounds so troubled that they were unable to take advantage of what we had to offer.

Then, several years ago, a day came when I was on a high. I had just enjoyed a stimulating breakfast in our nation's capital, at which I sat with the President of the United States. I left that breakfast and arrived at the airport for my return flight to New York. On the plane I picked up a copy of *The New York Times* and read an article that demonstrated to me that our ambitious "I Have a Dream Program" had indeed been worthwhile.

It was a front-page feature story about what was presumably the worst block in America. Unemployment, drugs, crime, depression, hopelessness—the block's residents lived with them every day. Of all the people mentioned in the article, only one had succeeded in making it out of the block. It was one of our Dreamers!

His father was a drug addict, and his mother, too. Early in his life, his family had broken up and he was raised by relatives for extended periods of time. He spent a large part of his childhood in squalid, horrid living conditions.

Everything was against him. Yet somewhere along the way, he made a decision. He must have said to himself, "This is not for me. I don't want this."

He was in a hopeless situation, but he made a decision. Since then, he has graduated from college and is beginning a career in the airline industry, possibly as a pilot. He made it. He's going to succeed.

I like to think that we played a role in his success, by making available to him some of the resources and opportunities he needed to overcome very high obstacles he faced in his life. We are so proud of him.

Yet he is not the only beneficiary of his success. Because of what he did, and the supporting role we played in it, we have overcome obstacles of our own, within our church community.

> *We've overcome the obstacle of negativity by seeing that, in our way, we can make a difference.*
>
> *We've overcome the obstacle of hopelessness, by seeing that we can help our city improve and grow stronger.*
>
> *We've shown ourselves that people are good and motivated and positive—people who come from any circumstances.*

So by helping people do their best, we have become better.

A simple thing to do, perhaps—one you can also do today. Strive to lift someone else. You will also lift yourself.

Take It One Day at a Time

When I feel immobilized by a task or problem that confronts me, I recall a principle developed by Sir William Osler, the great Canadian physician who lived in the early years of this century.

In a speech entitled "A Way of Life," which Dr. Osler delivered at Yale University in 1909, he explained his "practice of living for the day only, and for the day's work . . . in *day-tight compartments.*" And I find the concept so valuable that I'd like to share it with you.

In this speech, he relates that his "compartment" idea first came to him while he was riding on an ocean liner. A warning alarm sounded, and all the watertight compartments suddenly slammed tight below deck. He had a revelation: By concentrating solely on one day's work and shutting out other thoughts, it would be possible to get a day's work done without experiencing "mental distress, . . . worries about the future."

These words reflect the simple value of limiting worries about the future and simply living within the hours of today. Draw a circle, Dr. Osler said, around one twenty-four-hour period of time. Determine what you can do in that time, and don't bother your mind with worries about what you need to accomplish outside of that.

There are many examples of how this principle can be put to effective use in our lives.

I once heard the story of a tourist visiting a cathedral where an artisan was working on a huge mosaic. A vast empty wall was before the artist, and the tourist asked, "Aren't you worried about all that space that you need to fill up and how you will ever finish it?"

The artist replied simply that he knew what he could do in a day. Each morning, he marked off the area he would complete, and he didn't allow himself to worry about what lay outside that space. He just took one day at a time, and one day the mosaic would be finished.

Many of the great obstacles that stall our momentum are very much like that great, open wall. We can worry about the bigger picture we have to create. Or we can simply start to fill them with wonderful, unique images—the imprint of our lives—by doing the very best we can with each day we are given.

Where do you start? I offer a simple answer: The best place to start is wherever you are today.

Let Hope Pull You Through

I never gave up hope.

These words, or others very close to them, have been voiced by mountain climbers who lay in freezing crevices until their rescue, by people who have recovered from cancer, by people who survived the Great Depression, by soldiers who emerged alive from the most horrendous battles of this century.

Hope, which seems like the thinnest little thread, is really an incredibly powerful, dynamic force that can lead us from the most horrendous problems into a bright new day. Even the tiniest thread of hope, the most tender, provides a bridge from the darkness to the light.

Hang on to hope. Never give up on hope, no matter what, no matter how daunting the obstacles that lie in your path. It is your lifeline to the other side, because hope keeps possibility alive.

Let me share a personal memory. I remember taking a short walk into the woods several winters ago. It might have been the coldest night of the year, and I wanted the experience of being there among the trees for a few short minutes, relishing the absolute stillness. It must have been fifteen degrees below zero—but it was a calm, windless night.

I especially remember going up to one very thick, tall tree, which looked essentially dead. I tapped on it, and it felt and sounded dead, too. There was absolutely no feeling or sign of life in that tree.

I wondered, how can anything survive such frigid conditions? Yet I also knew that, deep in the heart of that tree, a life was waiting to burst open again in the spring. Invisible molecules were busily at work in anticipation of the first warm rays of sunshine. When that day came, the sap would flow again, the leaves would open. The whole organism would return to life. That tree wasn't dead. It was full of an infinite potential, much as we can be full of hope.

People who keep the faith—who hang on to hope—always emerge as victors. Like that tree, they are holding precious life alive deep within themselves.

If we can do that—no matter what obstacles confront us—we will bloom again.

Bring That Great Attitude
of Yours into Play

Are you confronting a daunting obstacle? How will you get around it?

There is no more powerful tool at your disposal—none!—than that great attitude we discussed together in the first chapter of this book.

When we opted for that good attitude, we determined so much of our destiny. What is attitude? Attitude is a mind set. It's the orientation of your mind or, better yet, the *direction* your mind is looking and going. It represents an entire way of positioning yourself in relationship to the outside world, and it determines the kind of life you will live.

And a good attitude doesn't look *to* life's obstacles. It looks *beyond* them.

People often talk about good attitudes and bad attitudes, and that's an important distinction to make. A good attitude is positive, affirming, open minded, and loving. It embodies a desire to learn and grow. A bad attitude, in contrast, is cynical, hopeless, helpless, unbending, unforgiving, closed minded, prejudiced—and unhappy. Given that kind of breakdown, we clearly see that your attitude colors the quality of your life.

But your attitude not only colors your life. It actually determines the content. A positive attitude keeps your life oriented toward growth beyond obstacles, because you continually strive for something a little higher, beyond your reach. A bad attitude leads you down a dead-end road of frustration and dissatisfaction.

You can pick either road. The choice is yours.

Ask Counsel,
But of the Right Person

Are you stalled by some seemingly insurmountable obstacle?

Try discussing your problem with someone whom you really trust—a person who has your best interests at heart. You are all but guaranteed to find ways to regroup and try to attack that problem in a different, more enlightened way.

But let me add a word of caution. Don't just ask anyone about the obstacles you're facing. Ask the *right* person.

Sounds simple, doesn't it? Yet bringing the right person into the process is not as easy as it seems. How can a willing, helpful person still be the wrong person to talk to? Let me share a simple example:

Paula was experiencing problems in her marriage. She was smart enough to realize that she needed support. So she called Susan, a friend who had been through a divorce the year before. Instead of really listening, Susan told Paula it was imperative to protect her financial assets, retain a good lawyer, investigate new schools for her children—and above all, move away from her husband as quickly as possible.

Now, Paula could have taken her friend's well-intentioned advice and acted upon it. Yet Paula was centered and aware enough to realize that Susan was mirroring—reflecting only her own problems and experiences onto her. And Paula was smart enough to say, "I may need the advice you are giving me at some point down the road, but it is too soon now. I'm asking for the personal support I need to save my marriage, not dissolve it." So Paula sought out the assistance of someone else—someone who asked questions first and was objective.

When you confront problems, that's the kind of person you should seek. Someone who comfortably fits into one or more of the following profiles:

- A good listener *who is objective enough to consider your own questions, concerns, and problems instead of trying to impose his or her own agenda.*

- A survivor *who has gone through something similar to what you are going through and emerged a victor. Possibly, someone who arrived at the outcome or success that most closely resembles the one your heart is hoping for.*

- *Someone who is not your* "world's biggest fan." *This may sound like a curious consideration. Yet the kind of person you are seeking should tell you more than,* "I love you, you're great, you can do anything!" *He or she should be able to help you confront personal limitations that may be holding you back. This confidant should be someone who can ask the "harder questions" that will empower you to confront self-limiting beliefs and get your life back on the momentum track.*

It may be a little more difficult, but you have to look for a right-minded person to help you get past the blockades and limitations of your life. If you look around you, chances are you know just who that person is, today.

Surrender the Problem

I think you'll agree that most of the insights we're sharing in this book are common sense and straightforward. There's nothing mysterious about them. They are plain and simple.

Well, now I'd like to share something mysterious with you. It's an unexpected way to get around life's obstacles. And for some reason, it really works—especially when you feel you have tried everything else to solve a problem and that you are on the point of defeat.

This solution is simply to *surrender*, to finally say, "The problem is bigger than anything I can handle. It's controlling me. I need help. I surrender."

It's interesting to reflect that, in twelve-step recovery programs, people sometimes say, "I surrender this problem to a higher power. It is beyond me." Doing so seems to serve as a vital step to moving ahead.

Surrender works. It could be that a higher power really does intercede when our personal wills fail. It could be that yielding breaks up the psychological log jam we've built around a problem. We can gain fresh insight and a less-cluttered mind.

Surrender, granted, might not be the first solution you try to a problem. It's something you apply down the line, when your personal and emotional resources have been tapped and you still cannot see a way around.

But it is an important step that, like prayer, invites something higher into the process. And when you find an approach that allows you to do that, my experience has shown me it's always an effective step to take.

Never Stop Trying

I remember when Dr. Norman Vincent Peale was in his seventies, he gave up one of his cherished summer vacations because he had a major problem to solve in one of his organizations.

There was some disbelief from his friends and associates. Many people said, "Why is it that this man, at this age and at this level of accomplishment, is still trying so hard?"

Dr. Peale left many inspiring concepts in the hearts and minds of his friends and followers. But for me, this may be the most inspiring of them all. And it is a good thought to keep close to our hearts:

Never give up.

No matter where you are in your life, never give up. Keep your momentum. And keep on striving.

CHAPTER THREE

Transform Your Life with Kindness

*Kindness is the golden chain
by which society is bound.*
— Goethe

When I am invited to give a speech, I often suggest a talk on kindness as one of my favorite topics. When I propose it, however, I sometimes sense a raised eyebrow and the thought, "A talk about *kindness*? Isn't it superficial? How about something a little more substantive?"

Yet when I give my talk about kindness, it doesn't take long for people to understand that kindness is more than just being nice. Kindness can be a life-transforming force. It is a gift we can give to everyone, ourselves included. It uplifts everyone as it uplifts ourselves.

There aren't many guarantees in life. In fact, there are very few. But this chapter offers you a guarantee that is as sure as any can be.

I guarantee this: If you take the one simple idea that you and I will share in this chapter and live with it to the heights and to the depths, the quality of your life will dramatically improve.

I also guarantee that your life will become not ordinary, but extraordinary in your eyes and the eyes of other people too. Your life will truly count for something and you will make a significant contribution to the world. When you die, you will be honored in a way my friend Laurie Beth Jones suggests: "May you live to be regretted by everyone."

What can bring about such a profound, guaranteed effect? It is kindness—plain, simple kindness. If you practice it, all those remarkable benefits, and many more, will enrich your life not just sometimes, but every day.

Be an Uplifting Force

Early one morning on my way to work, I stopped at a bank to use an ATM machine. As the door was closing behind me, I noticed a young woman running across the street toward me. I held the door another few seconds to let her in.

"Thank you very much, sir" she said to me.

There was only one machine working, and I finished making my transaction in less than a minute. By that time, several other people had lined up behind the woman. As I was walking away, she said, "Oh sir, do you have a pen I can use?"

And I said yes, and she took the pen and endorsed a check. In the moment it took her to do that, the man behind her waited patiently for her to finish. Like the rest of us, he was in a hurry to get his morning errands taken care of. Yet he did not move up to the machine. He waited. And when the woman was done endorsing her check, she said to him, "Thank you, sir, for waiting for me."

The whole exchange I have just described took a minute at most—maybe two. Yet during it, three strangers experienced a good feeling, an uplift. We were truly bound together by that common, golden chain of kindness.

No big deal, this little story? On the contrary. A very, very big deal indeed. Think if it had happened the other way—if we had all acted unkindly. Suppose I hadn't held the door, or she hadn't thanked me, or I'd refused to take a moment to lend her my pen, or the man had jumped ahead of her in line? Three people would have started their days with a sour taste in their mouths. Three people would have missed a little elation as they started out their days.

Yes, kindness is a big deal. It may not solve the biggest problems we're facing on any given day, but it might do something even more important. It might just equip us better to solve the problems we're facing.

Kindness frees us to do and act our best. It is one of the strongest motivators there is. It makes us just a little bit better than we would be otherwise—and a little more in tune with the world.

Each day, life presents us with many opportunities to take the higher road by thinking and acting kindly—or take the low road through unkind acts and thoughts. When you have that kind of choice, it is always wise to make the choice to be kind.

It's a simple way to transform your life and other people's too.

Lift Someone Today

The moment you enter the space occupied by a kind person, you feel a wonderful influence. You feel positive, elevated, inspired. Suddenly, new things are possible for you.

Several years ago, my wife Lea and I sensed kindness in just this way. We were attending a fund-raising event in the living room of an apartment on Fifth Avenue in New York. At one moment we found ourselves at opposite ends of the room. But even across that distance, we exchanged a significant look.

It was one of those moments when my wife knew exactly what was on my mind, and I knew what was on hers. Separately, we had spotted an elderly woman in that room who projected something extraordinary. She was not remarkably dressed, nor was she beautiful. She was simply an attractive older woman with a pleasant, wrinkled face and gray hair. But there was some positive energy there. Her face, in fact, glowed. She was radiant. My wife and I both wanted to get to know her.

Within a few minutes, we had worked our way through the crowd to her side, and we found out that she was everything we thought she might be.

We learned that both she and her husband had retired, from busy and demanding careers. She said they were enjoying their retirement in some special ways. One of the ways was through a game they played daily. She said it was called the "Lift Game." Through it, she and her husband tried to give a lift to people by showing kindness wherever they went—be it to a building doorman, a taxi driver, or a store clerk.

"We simply try to affirm people by being kind," she explained. "Then, when we're having dinner together at the end of the day, we talk about the 'lifts' that we gave to people during the day."

She mentioned an experience she had the day before. She was making a purchase in a department store. The clerk, a young woman, was sullen and downcast. She said, "I got a glimpse of her teeth and saw they were beautiful. I managed to get her to talk a bit, and then smile. When I saw her give a full smile, I saw how pretty she was, and I told her so. Her smile became broader and she came to life. That is a lift!"

She had been a professional woman and had made contributions during her working years. Now, she was continuing to make significant contributions—simply by excelling in kindness. As we talked with her, we sensed a presence that was not simply pleasant or charming. We realized we were in the presence of someone who was truly blessed, graced, and extraordinary.

That's not surprising, when you stop to think about it. When you practice kindness, you are not acting alone. You are joining in a powerful process. By practicing kindness, you become a medium for God's goodwill toward humanity.

What is kindness, after all, but a secondary means of grace? It is entering into partnership with the positive forces at work in the universe. I'd challenge you to think of a more significant role, or more powerful one, to take with your life.

Cultivate a Forgiving Heart

One of the greatest stories, not only in the Bible but also in all of literature, I believe, is the description of an incident that occurred early one morning as Jesus was teaching. Some religious leaders—scribes and Pharisees, as the story says—brought forward a woman who had been caught in the act of adultery.

These accusers were hard-line legalists, eager to challenge Jesus. They were bothered by his teachings on love and forgiveness, and to test him, they challenged him on the letter of the law, saying, "The Law of Moses says that anyone caught in adultery should be stoned. What do you say? What is your judgment?"

The story relates that Jesus got down on his knees and wrote something in the sand. What he wrote was not recorded—perhaps he was only buying a little time to think or to let the tension of the moment dissipate.

Then he stood up and looked each person in the eye. My guess is that each look was a *long* one. Then he said, "Anybody here who has never sinned—*you* throw the first stone."

There was a long silence. Then one by one they turned away and left.

Only the distraught and frightened woman remained behind. Jesus looked at her and said, "Where are they? Is there no one to accuse you?"

She replied, "No, they have all gone."

Jesus said, "Neither do I accuse you. Go—but don't sin anymore."

Jesus, we see, did not agree with or condone what the woman might have done. But neither did he judge. He was kind, and he understood. And with his understanding heart, he literally *freed* her.

The message in this story, we know, goes beyond questions of sin and pardon. It tells us that the better path in our lives is to forgive, not to judge. It counsels us to set aside our own opinions and direct a constant stream of kindness at others—even when we do not act as they do or condone their actions.

It counsels us to have something better than judgment or opinions. And that "something" is a forgiving heart.

A forgiving heart can free other people, as the woman was freed in the story from the Bible. But just as importantly, it can help us free ourselves.

Learn to Empathize

Empathy is an extraordinarily focused type of kindness.

To have empathy is to *feel with* another person. I know that no one can feel exactly as someone else does at any given moment, especially when that other person is in pain, or acting aggressively, or simply not communicating. Yet even when such obstacles are present, we can still empathize—*feel with*—that other person. And we can be kind.

The results of simple, kind empathy can be remarkable.

Some years ago my secretary, Gerd Gunnelfson, interrupted a meeting I was conducting to say our receptionist had just called. A very distraught man had entered the lobby of the church, asking to see a minister. Because every minister was occupied, and I was busy too, I said, "I'll go down as soon as I am free. But if it is really serious, I'll come sooner."

I expected to get a call within a few minutes. But none came. My meeting finished, I was not called to the lobby, and I resumed my work. Nearly an hour later, Gerd returned. I asked how the situation in the lobby had been resolved.

She said, "The man has calmed down and is all right. He said he no longer needed to see a minister."

And Gerd had handled the situation on her own.

I asked her what she did. She said, "I decided to go down to the lobby. On the way down, I tried to get centered within myself and get calm. My idea was to try to carry that feeling over into the situation I was about to enter. When I got down there, the man was really agitated. But I sat silently with him. I didn't say much. I was simply trying to feel what he felt at the moment, to empathize with him in his emotional state and direct feelings of calm his way."

Her silence created an atmosphere that helped him feel safe with himself. And finally, he got back in control, and he felt calmer. Most remarkably, she had accomplished all that without saying many words or asking the man to explain his troubles.

Empathy has that kind of power—to cut through other people's pain silently, as an act of caring kindness.

Affirm Someone with Kindness

Affirm someone else.

When you affirm, you are blessing. You are trying to hold someone up—enhance someone.

You can affirm people, even when you disagree with them or have trouble understanding what they are going through at the time. Affirmation is a wonderful, active way to be kind.

I think back to a time when I was a freshman at college. That year was horrendous for me. I had come from a small city where most of my activities took place within a mile's radius of my home. I felt safe and secure, surrounded by people I had known all my life.

Then I went off to a college nearly a thousand miles away. I didn't know how to handle myself. How frightened I was. I harbored a growing fear that I might flunk out.

The turnaround came one day during my second semester, on a day when my English professor was returning some essay papers to the class. She held mine up, and I could see all the red marks and comments she had put on it. I thought, "Oh, what is she going to do? Criticize my work in front of all these other students?"

Instead, she said, "Your grammar and spelling need a lot of work, Arthur, but this is an example of a very well-organized paper."

Surely she had no idea what she had done for me. She had blessed me with an affirmation. She had shown me I could do something.

I knew I could organize thoughts and put them into a sequence. There was a chance for me. Maybe I would not flunk out. Maybe I could make it after all. And many times afterward, remembering that kindness helped me press on.

Even small acts of affirmation are that powerful. They bring out the best in people and help them bring the full measure of their goodness into the world.

Compare affirmation with negative judgment—the other side of the coin—which is destructive both to you and to those you judge.

How many times, after all, are we tempted to put people down—to show up their shortcomings, to put them down in order to make ourselves feel, for a moment, superior? Yet we can choose not to follow that path. As the Bible says, "Judge not, that you be not judged. Condemn not, that you be not condemned."

With kindness and affirmation, you can direct a greater love everywhere.

Lift Up the World

Unkindness is not a minor or unimportant problem in the world. In fact, sociologists and psychologists tell that children of abusive families are more likely to be abusive parents in their adult years. Conversely, the children of kind families become kind parents themselves.

When unkindness affects a society, a significant portion of that population becomes troubled, dysfunctional, unkind, violent—and a burden to everyone else. So kindness and unkindness are the two sides of a very keen sword.

Some years ago, noted author Elisabeth Kübler-Ross spoke at the Marble Collegiate Church. In her talk, she explained that we all have a dark side, which she labeled "The Hitler Within." It was harrowing and revelatory to hear this brilliant woman explain how each of us does, in fact, embody a very dangerous potential for evil—a tendency that demands our awareness and vigilance.

Yet, as she pointed out, we can win this battle.

History tells us that kindness is more powerful than hatred. Evil may win out for a time, but kindness always wins out over aggression, mean-spiritedness, hatred, bigotry, and the other dark forces. Those forces sometimes gain an upper hand in the ebb and flow of history and events. But in time, the bad forces lose out to love, respect, and the higher human virtues.

Kindness is a good place to start fighting for the good and combating the evil in the world.

Think small. Get started. Take simple, immediate steps each day that lie within your power.

Simply exercise kindness in your next human encounter, sense the good in that act, and keep going. Once you've started, the world's work is well underway.

Start a Ripple Effect

Like the ripples that begin when a stone is tossed into a still lake, kindness ripples into every corner of our lives, bounces off everything and everyone—and returns to us bearing surprising rewards and enrichment.

Not long ago I had lunch with a woman who is a healer. She's a legitimate, professional healer, who has shown an ability to lay on hands and help people overcome pain and illness. She mentioned that, after our lunch, she would be driving to Pennsylvania to visit a horse farm. I was unprepared for her reason for going. She said that day would be her fourth visit to do a laying-on of hands . . . with horses!

She was absolutely serious. In fact, she told me she was achieving some remarkable results.

She told me that the owners of the farm had called her because they were experiencing problems with several very troubled animals. Some were acting very aggressively. The trainers, expert though they were, hadn't been able to solve the problem. Veterinarians had visited, but they couldn't find any physical reasons for the behavior.

Everyone had thrown up their hands. There was something wrong that they could not identify. In frustration, the owners of that farm decided to call a healer. Nothing else had helped, so why not try?

When she arrived at the farm for her first visit, she saw that everything she had been told was true. There was chaos among the horses. They were agitated, hard to control. Yet as she watched, she could sense that one horse was clearly the most aggressive and troubled of them all.

She decided to start her work with that horse. How? She actually took him aside and did a laying-on of hands with him. She talked to him and she prayed. By her second visit, that horse had begun to calm down. It became evident that her efforts were beginning to help. By her third visit, all the horses seemed to recognize her and quiet down as soon as she arrived. The situation really was much better, to the point that normal training routines could resume.

You can logically attribute her success to many factors. You might correctly conclude that animals have feelings and like to be treated well. You might decide that once the behavior of the most aggressive horse was altered, a new balance could be achieved within the group. It's even possible to conclude that when the trainers saw the most aggressive horse in control, they felt better able to do their jobs.

All those conclusions are valid, but they were all triggered by kindness, the gentle act of a healing touch.

As I say, kindness works with a ripple effect. Apply a little somewhere in your life and you have little way of knowing how many lives can be affected, how many troubling situations will improve—at times miraculously.

Be Kind, With a Pure Heart

Whatever your faith may be, I expect that you believe that God's kindness knows no boundaries—it is not restricted to certain people only. And neither, I think, should our kindness be directed to a small group of chosen people.

Yet it seems to be part of human nature to set up boundaries and divisions, even deciding who is worthy of receiving kindness from us.

"I've been stung too many times in my relationships," a young woman told me recently. "I've had it with being kind toward everyone. People only take advantage of me, so I'm getting my defenses up."

She was, I think, suffering under a misunderstanding of what it means to be kind. Being kind doesn't mean you are weak. It doesn't mean you have no standards or boundaries. It doesn't mean you fail to differentiate right from wrong or that you allow people to take advantage of you.

Kindness means that no matter what happens to you, you take the high road. You do not respond with aggression, even when you are confronted by it. You do not respond to meanness or pettiness in kind.

You've surely observed that, if someone expects a fight and you respond with kindness, you can often break down their defenses and sometimes even take the wind out of their sails. Acting aggressively rarely accomplishes such things.

Cultivating a mean heart is not a way to prevent yourself from being hurt. It is just a way of inflicting hurt upon yourself and others at the same time—and diminishing the quality of everyone's life.

Don't Take Things Out on People

I have known many troubled relationships in which the husband and wife vent their frustrations and anger the moment they see each other at the end of every day. They bicker and exchange verbal jabs.

In other, more stable marriages, the husband and wife make a point to set aside their daily frustrations. They may share the same problems and even a degree of differences, yet they have the wisdom to be kind with each other. They may touch, hug, and utter kind words.

They may then go on to discuss the issues they need to deal with—problems that are part of any relationship—yet they know that they stand a better chance of being happy if they choose to be kind and civil to one another. They don't take things out on each other.

You needn't be in a great mood, after all, to act with kindness. Even grumpy people can still be kind. You need only resist the temptation to indulge frustrations and blow off steam.

Which path will you choose? Unkindness is a simple path to follow, but it might finally corrupt the quality of the relationships you need and value the most. It's just as simple to take the kinder, higher road and claim the rewards that await you there.

Again, Take the Higher Road

If you look back to your childhood, you can find some memory of other people's kindnesses and unkindnesses to you. You carry the emotional scars of the effects of unkind people. And you also carry the joy and power lent to you by extraordinarily kind people who elevated you and empowered you and changed your life by simply being kind. Thus we know very well the impact of human kindness and unkindness.

Why is it, then, when we grow, we sometimes allow ourselves to be influenced by people who operate at the lowest common denominator? Can we not begin to speak out, using even the simple words *kindness, courtesy, hospitality,* and *honor*? Can we not affect the lives of young people, and all other people around us, by becoming leaders in kindness— and in the uplifting of the human spirit?

Go forth in the ministry of goodness and love. Start today, by simply being kind.

CHAPTER FOUR

Welcome Stillness into Your Life

For centuries, spiritually oriented people have sought out silent places to experience the divine and the heavenly. In fact, many people say they can experience the divine only in a state of quiet. It is clear that the wisdom of the ages encourages a movement toward stillness and quiet.

Yet our society seems to be going in the opposite direction. Like a snowball going down a hill, we're hurtling into a world that seems ever louder, more frenzied, and more distracting.

How can we find inner stillness and silence in the midst of such hectic days?

There is good news. We can find quiet and stillness in our lives—even when our phones are ringing, our work life seems chaotic, and our senses are under a constant barrage.

We can do it. *You* can do it.

We can do it by doing what people have done for centuries, tapping our inner resources of stillness and calm. I believe that quiet is at the center of the universe. And a quiet stillness also resides at the center of our being.

Tapping your inner quiet is a simple step that can drastically improve the quality of your life. And, just like claiming a positive attitude or living a life of kindness, it is based on a simple decision that, once made, can transform the quality of your life.

Seek Out Your Quiet Spaces

I spend my summer vacations in Maine. I have an annual ritual that is a staple of my life. On one of the last days before I return to New York and my busy new season of work, I rise long before dawn, go down to the dock, and pilot my boat out of the sight of land. Alone there, I wait for the sunrise.

On those days, I am totally alone. There is absolute stillness, except for the sound of water lapping against the side of the boat or the early morning call of a gull.

Then, it happens. The day is born. There is no sound, just an amazing moment when the edge of the sun meets the horizon, its orb explodes into the sky and brings a sudden warmth. It is awesome. It's like being present at the creation of the world.

It *is* being present at creation. It is the beginning of a new day. And the whole possibility of the new day is born in complete stillness.

When I allow myself this experience, I am keenly aware that I am recording it for the winter months that lie ahead. In my mind's eye, I will return to it often.

It is a private moment I will revisit many times when I feel myself drawn into the noise, stress, and hectic pace of living in a city. I go back there, and it sustains me. This is my private practice of silence. And it's a practice that's available to you, too.

How can you get started with your own discipline of silence? I'd urge you to start by identifying personal quiet places you already know. Recall them as vividly as you can, and learn to call up the feeling of calm and quiet they evoke in you. You might choose to recall any quiet, restful moment that's in your memory. It might be the quiet you experienced last week while you were working in your yard. Or perhaps the peace you felt during a moment of silence during religious services.

You'll find that you can call up the sensations and feelings of those places and experience again the calm they bring.

Then I'd urge you to take the next step, to cultivate new quiet experiences, like my sunrise routine. Select some quiet, calm place and live in it fully for even a brief time. Imprint it on your mind, so you can call it up again and again—whenever and wherever you need it—so that you can enjoy a moment of inner calm and quiet stillness.

This is your *gathering* of silence.

Next, let's look at another key way to gather silence into your life, by making it a part of your daily routine.

Make Silent Time
Part of Every Day

 The Twenty-Third Psalm, in its great wisdom, describes an ideal context for silence and contemplation:

He makes me to lie down in green pastures, he leads me beside the still waters, he restores my soul.

What an inspiring depiction of a peaceful, quiet setting in which to be alone. The green pasture, with warm sunshine and cool breezes, the mirrorlike surface of still water, all provide just the right context for restoring our souls.

We'd all love to go to a place like that. Yet how many of us can find such a place to go to during the course of each day? Very few.

We know that making time to be quiet isn't always easy. But that doesn't mean it's impossible.

I have a friend named Susan who has three children and a very demanding job as a minister of a large inner-city church. Yet she nonetheless sits quietly in a chair for fifteen minutes each day, enjoying her private minutes of meditation and prayer.

She'd certainly be justified in saying, "My life is pulled in too many directions to allow me to indulge in such time for myself. I have young children and things to do."

Yet her children and husband have all learned to respect "Mommy's quiet time." People, after all, will sense and respect other people's needs to be quiet.

I'd encourage you, too, to find time for quiet in your daily routine. It might be during your commuting time, in a small parcel of time you set aside in the early morning or before going to sleep late at night—even over your lunch hour at work. I know one man who goes to his local library to be quiet or, weather permitting, to the park.

I have a friend who has a half-hour subway ride each morning and—believably or unbelievably—he makes his quiet time in the midst of that noise and movement.

You don't need much time to gather into yourself a peaceful feeling of calm and quiet.

Now, once you begin to set aside that quiet time, what should you do with it? As you sit there alone and still, won't you be troubled and distracted by the nervous activity of your mind?

That's a very telling question, of course. And the answers to it are not as simple as many people might expect.

I recall an experience I had many summers ago in England. While I was staying at a country inn, I became aware that the silence around me was absolute, as complete as I had ever experienced. There was no sound of any kind. There were no crickets or katydids, no cars passing by, no refrigerator running in the next room. Nothing.

I was delighted as I went to bed, expecting that I would find some profound sense of relaxation and calm. Yet when I got into bed, my body felt tense and tight. All kinds of thoughts kept intruding into the silence I was so looking forward to—thoughts about bills to pay, travel arrangements to make, work left undone.

Even though I cherished that stillness, I didn't know how to handle it. I had found silence, but I didn't know what to do with it. It wasn't working for me.

When this happens to you, what should you do?

Focus on the silence. Concentrate on the quiet. Enter into the stillness. Keep it all simple.

This can be difficult to accomplish since our tendency is to bring our busyness into the quiet. We mentally utter many words and juggle many thoughts.

The key is simplifying—uncomplicating our minds.

Traditionally, when we encounter silence, whether in prayer, or meditation, or simply when surrounded by silence, we feel the need to say something, to ask something. And too often, this is done with too many thoughts and words. After all, we are conditioned to complicate things. Yet the mystics of the ages offer wise counsel. They say that when we enter silence, we do not need many words. We can do well with just one word. For ages sages have done well by saying, "God . . . God . . . God . . . God."

Similarly, many people who meditate use a repeated word known as a *mantra.*

Another step? To simply *listen.* Listen to your inner voice. Listen to the moment. Listen to the quiet. When we learn to be still and simply listen restfully, we allow ourselves to hear new things.

Consider these words, written by the polar explorer Admiral Richard Byrd. They beautifully describe an experience he had at the South Pole.

Take your time and read slowly and thoughtfully:

I paused to listen to the silence. My breath crystallized as it passed my cheeks. Drifted on a breeze gentler than a whisper. My frozen breath hung like a cloud overhead. The day was dying, the night was being born, but with great peace. And here were the imponderable processes and forces of the cosmos, harmonious and soundless.

Harmony, that it was. That was what came out of the silence. A gentle rhythm. The train of a perfect chord. The music of the spheres, perhaps. It was enough to catch that rhythm momentarily to be myself a part of it. I could feel no doubt of man's oneness with the universe, and the conviction came that that rhythm was too orderly, too harmonious, too perfect to be a product of blind chance. That there must be a purpose in the whole and that man was part of the whole and not an accidental offshoot. It was a feeling that transcended reason, that went to the heart of man's despair and found it groundless. The universe was a cosmos, not a chaos. Man was rightfully a part of that cosmos as were the day and night.

That's what Admiral Byrd discovered in silence. You might experience silence differently—yet the likelihood is that you will discover the order and rhythm of the universe. If you make silence part of your life, you will find something that is reassuring, meaningful, refreshing—uniquely your own.

Part of the process is what you bring to it—an agreement and commitment to set aside part of your day to being quiet and still, even in the noisiest and most hectic part of your day. The rest? Something magical and surprising that is contributed not by you, but by the power of the silence itself.

But we're not describing the kind of magic that you can wait for, and that never comes. This kind of magic does come. You can call it into your life, every day, by giving yourself one simple gift. Just be quiet and listen.

Let Silence Deepen Love

The effectiveness of silence to improve human relationships is well documented. I know one successful businessperson who counts silence and listening among his most effective tools for running a business. He explains:

> When someone in the company comes to me and is upset and bothered by something, I always sit quietly and allow that person as much time as needed to say everything that's on his or her mind—everything. I quiet my own mind and avoid the all-too-human tendency to formulate a response or rebuttal while the other person is speaking. The other person needs to sense my attention and feel that I'm really hearing every word. This is the first step toward clear communication.

Simply listening is often the first step toward improving human friendships and relationships.

Have you ever noticed that people who find it difficult to listen to each other quietly, are often having trouble in other areas of their relationship as well? I'm often struck that when marriages or other love relationships become troubled, both parties feel uncomfortable in periods of silence, not reassured and supported by the presence of the other person.

Some couples have difficulty accomplishing that. Each partner gets mired in thoughts such as, "What is he (or she) thinking, why isn't he (or she) saying anything?"

On the other side of the coin, haven't we all seen couples who seem to be completely silent and at home with each other, going about their life together in complete comfort and quiet harmony? Such relationships offer one of life's most joyous sights.

Well, why not for you, too?

It is never too late to bring the healing power of silence and listening into a relationship—even a troubled one where there might be blame, miscommunication, and friction.

Be quiet and listen to each other. You will revitalize both your lives.

Express Kindness through Silence

Keeping silent and listening can be your greatest gift to others.

Recall times when somebody really heard you, and consider the difference it made. And then recall other times when you needed another person to hear you, and that somebody didn't. Remember how hurt and limited you felt.

When you are heard, you can be healed. Several years ago a woman named Linda visited my office. She was visibly upset, and I began to ask her what was wrong and how I could help her. I was surprised when she told me, "I just want to sit here in silence."

So we did that. I found it difficult at first since I wanted to hear her problems, offer advice, and possibly help resolve whatever was wrong. But I saw that she really wanted me to simply be present for her.

So we sat in silence, which seemed to become steadily more profound. Not one word was said. At last, she told me that she had gotten the help she needed, and she left. Some time later, she told me that our time together had been "a significant moment" in her life and "a turning point." Ever since, she sends me notes from time to time to let me know how her life is moving forward.

So silence may not be as passive as it seems. It can be an *active* way to help others.

There is a book called *A Listening Ear,* a collection of essays by Paul Tournier, the Swiss psychiatrist. In this book, the author describes himself as a shy and awkward teenager. Like many young people who are struggling to define themselves and their place in the world, he even termed himself "odd."

Then, when Tournier was sixteen, one of his teachers invited this awkward young student to his home, wanting to do something positive to help this shy and awkward youngster. And it worked.

According to Tournier, that day marked the first validation of his worth and humanity. "On that day," Tournier writes, "I began to exist."

And what was the conversation like between Tournier and his teacher? As Tournier recalls, they discussed nothing monumental. It was simply the first time he felt someone really *listened* to what he had to say. He expressed something about himself, his views, his ambitions—and his life began to move ahead, simply because someone else was on the receiving end of his ideas.

Too often, after all, we talk past each other, engaging in separate monologues. Each of us wants to be heard, but no one hears. Yet we can break the cycle with the simple act of silent, still attentiveness. Listening is one of the most effective ways we can show caring and love.

Silent listening shows care, and it can therefore be a highly effective way to deal with people in moments of crisis. Let me share a story of just how effective silence can be.

Once at Marble Collegiate Church, we were hosting a memorial service for Chiang Kai Shek. The church was full of dignitaries. As Dr. Norman Vincent Peale, my predecessor, was speaking, a woman in the balcony suddenly began to speak out loudly, audibly responding to Dr. Peale's remarks. She even cheered, "Go, Norman! That's right! Go, Norman!"

Obviously, somebody had to do something. I happened to be seated near this woman, and I went and sat quietly on the balcony step near her seat. I caught her eye and gestured very silently, without saying a word. She responded by becoming very quiet and mimicking my gestures. She was obviously a sad, disturbed individual. Yet I was shortly able to get her to follow me out of the sanctuary, without saying a word.

So our silence and ability to listen can be an effective way to calm others by expressing, without speaking a word, our care and concern.

Listening to someone doesn't require special training or abilities. Whether it's with a person you know well, or someone you are meeting for the first time, you can express that wonderful, silent care. Watch as it transforms both your days, and possibly your life as well.

Share Silent Rituals
and Support

Let's share a moment of silence.

Those words, for me, bring an immediate sensation of calm and peace.

I'd like to ask you to pause a moment and think about moments of silence you have shared with other people. Perhaps you will recall a silent grace before a family Thanksgiving or the moment of communal silence during a service of worship. You might even recall the moment of silence you might have shared with other members of a team just before playing an important game or a special silent moment with someone you deeply love.

When people experience silence together, something remarkable happens. They sense a deeper, profound connection with "something bigger"—a presence or even a spirit that imbues that moment and their lives with a special quality that transcends everyday life. There is a special bonding.

Religions have long utilized this unique power of communal silence. I am always struck by its power when I attend a Quaker meeting, which I do at least once a year as part of my regular spiritual practice. Each time I do, I am reminded of the power of silence within a worship context.

As you may know, Quakers have no preaching or singing in their services. The meeting room where they convene is plain, with no embellishment. Chairs or benches are arranged in a circle, and people speak only when they feel moved "by the spirit" to say something. Usually what is said is brief, thoughtful, and personal.

There is more quiet than speaking. Sometimes, people sit for an hour or more in complete silence, nobody saying a word. These services are among the most memorable and meaningful for me.

Let me relate my own story about the spiritual power of silence.

Up until a few years ago, people in the congregation at the Marble Collegiate Church had the regular routine of entering the sanctuary before services and chatting and talking in a friendly way right up until the moment the service started. The man who was organist at the time decided to discontinue his practice of playing musical preludes during that period, noting that people who hadn't seen each other for a week needed time to catch up. Many people commented on the level of chatter, some honoring it, others wishing something could be done to limit it.

But then a man from the congregation offered a helpful idea. He said, "I understand all this talk, but I find that I need quiet to *prepare* for worship. I need to get centered. What about having a three-minute period of silence before we begin our worship?"

With some apprehension, I instituted the new procedure. I was anxious about the response, as people generally resist changing old routines.

The result, however, was phenomenal. I expected that I would have to make an announcement each week, "We will now observe three minutes of silence until worship begins." But I only had to make that announcement twice. Now, silence is a central part of our routine. At the moment the ministers enter the church, the congregation quiets, and sometimes three minutes is not long enough.

This is our period of corporate quiet. It centers everyone and prepares them for the experience that is about to follow. And now it has become an integral part of our communal experience each week.

There are many times when the experience of being part of a silent group heightens our awareness of purpose, of life's deeper meanings—or simply of our support and love for other people when they need us to be there.

A young man I know recalls this experience from his youth:

> *I was only about fourteen years old when my family's physician died suddenly. Because he and his family were Jewish, my parents knew that his wife and family would be observing the practice known as "sitting Shiva." They would simply open their home and allow all visitors to come in. It was one of my first encounters with grief and mourning and, as I apprehensively put on my suit and tie, I expected that I would be entering a place that would be dominated by great emotional turmoil.*
>
> *I was worried! What would I say to my doctor's widow? What would I say to his children, who were my friends? Would I offend people by doing the wrong thing as part of this Jewish ritual? I was uncomfortable with the thought that I might offend people in this public expression of grief I would not understand.*
>
> *I was completely unprepared for what we found when we arrived at the house and went in. There were probably thirty-five people seated in the living room in complete silence around the bereaved family. Christian and Jew, we were all united in a bond of silent caring, concern and sorrow. I saw that my silent presence there*

was all that was required at that moment. In my silence, I was saying something that could comfort the family in its worst moment. In my silence I was speaking powerfully about my care for that family and expressing my own grief.

How familiar those words seem to me. In my own childhood in a predominately Italian community, I recall entering homes where someone had died. I remember seeing elderly women just sitting there, not uttering a word. They sat in total and complete silence, dressed in their black dresses. I remember the power that such a silent presence had to draw other people into it—to make groups of people sit enveloped in complete and total quiet. Yet in that silence, people were really saying, "We are here with you. We share, in this common silent space, your experience and pain."

When you can, where you can, find quiet time with other people. You will immediately add a new, deeper dimension to the experience of living.

Let Silence
Open Your Creative Mind

How often have you confronted a problem that required your creativity—a problem that would not respond to hard work alone? No matter how hard you would bear down, you felt stuck and unable to move ahead.

Please know that creative activities are not only for artists, writers, and creative geniuses. We all face challenges every day that require great creativity. We need to find the right words to say to a child who is facing a problem. On the job, we need to hit upon just the right approach to get the people we work with to solve problems or rise to a new level of performance.

Life is full of problems that demand creative solutions. And I'd like to share with you a secret solution to finding them that I've found and tested out time and time again. It works, and it is simple. It is silence.

I know as much about feeling creative block as anyone ever could. After all, in nearly every week of my life, for many years, I've been faced with a very particular kind of creative project: writing a weekly sermon. And as someone has aptly said, writing and delivering a sermon is really creating a work of art.

For years, I was frustrated and critical of myself as I went through the process. It was a real ordeal for me. I would write for ten or fifteen minutes, then leave my desk to do this or that. I'd get a cup of tea or coffee, make a phone call, do a little chore, or even take a walk.

I thought I was just wasting time, that I was avoiding the challenge of writing and creating. What was going on? Why was I wasting so much time? Why couldn't I sit down and just write the sermon? Why was I avoiding the work at hand by allowing myself to be distracted?

Then it hit me. I wasn't avoiding the work at hand. I was engaged in a creative process. I wasn't being lazy. My mind was trying to tell me that in order to work creatively, it needed breaks—periods of silence and quiet reflection during which my subconscious mind could work.

So I started to consciously allow silence and quiet into the creative process, all but "shutting out" thoughts of the creative problem I was facing for minutes at a time while I enjoyed mental quiet and let my mind unwind.

And this creative process works. Now, each time I return to my sermon writing, I've gained new insights, a new perspective, and also new realizations about where I might have made a wrong decision or taken a wrong turn with an idea.

Incidentally, I also realized that complete silence is required while I am writing or pursuing any other creative activity; music or a TV or radio playing in the background immediately reduces the ability of my mind to engage in creative, free thought.

Apply silence and flexibility to the next creative challenge you face, and watch the results. You will discover, as I have, that creativity is directly tied to your ability to be quiet and still in the time in and around your work.

Angels Passing Over

Not long ago, I was enjoying the company of a large group of people at a special dinner.

It was often a boisterous, noisy evening. Yet I happened to notice, on a couple of occasions, a rather remarkable phenomenon.

At least two or three times during the evening, there was a sudden and eery quiet. Everyone stopped talking at the same time. Aware of the phenomenon, people stared at each other with a sense of wonder, then resumed their conversation.

Someone once described this very phenomenon as "an angel passing over."

That's a very charming and interesting notion. It means that when an angel passes, people are silent, even though they don't know why. And then, once the angel has passed, they continue their conversation.

Whether the silence that passes over us *and into us* is an angel or something else may well remain a mystery.

What is not a mystery, however, is that silence is not a simple absence of noise. When conversation stops and inhabits a room as if by magic, we see that silence is not a nothing, but a *something*—a palpable entity we can inhabit. It can ease our life, enrich it, and build a connection to other people.

Silence, often overlooked, enriches our lives. And claiming its rich rewards is not a complex or difficult task.

Silence is free for the asking.

CHAPTER FIVE

Settle with the Past and Move On

We are products of everything that has ever happened to us—a sum total of all our successes, failures, disappointments, and triumphs. Our childhoods are still with us every day. So are our mothers, our fathers, all the people who had a part in raising us, and—to a greater or lesser extent—every person we have ever known.

Who we are today is a combination of all the experiences we have had and all the reactions we have had to them.

Yet does our past determine our future? To some extent, but not entirely. There's something even more important than the past we've had. It's our *reaction and response* to those experiences.

In other words, what counts is *how effectively we are dealing with the past.*

Many of us run a real danger of becoming crippled by the past, unable to move beyond it. And if that happens, we become its prisoner. I am continually amazed at the number of people I have talked with—people in their seventies, eighties, and even nineties—who remain stuck in their childhood traumas.

That needn't happen to us. As we grow and mature, we have a choice to make. We can choose to remain victims of the past or learn to deal with our earlier lives in a way that serves us, not cripples us. We can find ways to learn and grow from everything that has ever happened to us.

Whether your past has been happy or sad, troubled or calm, today is a new day. It is a chance to move on. In the pages that follow, you and I will share what can be a wonderful experience—the cathartic one of letting go and making a new start in life.

As in the other simple steps in this book, we must work at our problems, continually evaluating and striving to stretch and grow. But rest assured, tomorrow will be much different if you can carry through on the ideas we will share here.

Move Beyond Problems

We all know people who are not at peace with their past. They're unable to let go of life's setbacks and disappointments. They often blame themselves for their problems, pointing to ways they have messed up their lives. Or they direct blame at parents, spouses, relatives, teachers or even strangers who have hurt them.

These people seem to require profound repair and redirection. Often it is imperative to work with a good therapist in this process, as I chose to do. One thing I have learned is that no problem ever goes away on its own. For any human obstacle to be overcome, there must be inner work.

We all have a choice to make, a decision to solve problems and move on, or live with them and allow them to beat us down for the rest of our lives. We need to state it again: There is only one way to solve a problem—to work on solving it. Problems don't just go away.

Let me share some personal truths with you.

My mother was a very good woman and homemaker, yet she was emotionally very fragile. Since she was not emotionally available to my brothers or me, she left us wanting. In fact, I was well along with my life before I realized that my relationship with her might have been at the root of many of the problems that were presenting themselves to me in my middle age.

My first signal that something was wrong was a serious illness. My arteries got clogged and I required bypass surgery. Afterwards, my surgeon recommended me to a psychiatrist. After working with him for several weeks, I summoned up some courage and asked, "I know *what* went wrong with me, but can you tell me *why* it happened? Why did I get sick?"

His answer was almost too quick, but it was right on target, reminding me of the connection of mind and body. His exact words to me were, "Arthur, you know that this didn't just happen."

He next said, "Clogged-up arteries are from clogged-up emotions."

Then he said, "All the people I have worked with on this problem have two major things going on in their lives. One is repressed hostility. The other is feeling trapped."

As quickly as he spoke these words, I knew he was right. I had never learned to identify my anger or find healthy ways to express it. And I felt trapped in several important relationships.

I had a choice to make. I could either remain stuck in those problems, or do the work I needed to do to get beyond them.

Notice, I'm not speaking here of simply "letting go" of problems. Even "letting go" takes hard work. We can't just think anger away. We must get in touch with its source, what it means, and find healthy ways of dispersing it. None of us can simply "will" emotional health when it has been wanting. It is necessary to identify the lacks and losses, talk them through, and find healthy relationships to help meet present needs.

In a book about "Simple Steps," this step might seem puzzling. It might be simple to take, but the walk may be trying and painful. Solving some problems takes energy and a long-term investment of time.

Yet I was surprised to find that one simple step did get the process started. I told myself, "I am determined to get past these problems and move on." It took me several years of therapy, but in the end, it was liberating and energizing for me.

As the author Scott Peck observed, "The only way to solve a problem is to *solve* it." In other words, we must empower ourselves to move forward.

It is remarkable that, when we give ourselves permission to do that, many problems we've dealt with on a daily basis lose their power to unnerve us. Problems become what they should be—opportunities to stretch and grow, to become wiser and stronger. They gradually become a part of life that enriches our understanding and deepens our awareness of how wonderful it can be to move ahead and grow as we progress on this earthly journey called life.

Make a Fresh Start
Each Day

In the book of Genesis, we find the story of Sodom and Gomorrah and Lot's wife.

That story relates that the cities Sodom and Gomorrah had become evil and decadent and that God was about to destroy them because of the ruinous lives their citizens had chosen to lead. However, as the story goes, God looked favorably at Lot and his family because, of all the inhabitants, they were righteous and good. So Lot and his family were given a chance to leave the city before it was destroyed.

The only requirement? They could not look back at the city as they walked away from it.

Of course, you know the story of Lot's wife. She looked back and was destroyed—turned into a pillar of salt. She was unable to leave her ties to her past and move on.

This story from the Bible bears a close resemblance to the Greek myth of Orpheus. A mortal, he was permitted to journey into the underworld and bring his beloved Eurydice back from the dead—provided that he resist the temptation to look back at her as she followed him back into the living world. But he was unable to resist the temptation, and when he turned around, she was snatched back into Hades.

We can view these stories as allegories for what happens when we need to move ahead in our lives but are unable to shed the baggage of the past or move beyond relationships, habits, lifestyles, and behavior that is unhealthy and destructive. If we don't look ahead, we can find ourselves stuck and frozen in place.

The moral of these stories may well be that no matter how strongly we feel drawn to live in the past—even a dreadful one, like Hell itself or the awful life that Lot and his wife were leaving behind—we need to discipline ourselves to keep moving ahead.

This is a choice we all have to make—to move beyond past problems and past hurts.

We all have the power to turn toward the future and away from the past. It is a critical first step toward a better life.

Accept the Irony
That Life Is Unfair, But Good

I'd like you to ponder a big mystery with me, a contradiction.

Life is unfair. Yet life is good.

Our ability to thoughtfully and creatively deal with the unfairness and build on the good can make the difference between a happy or unhappy life.

One reason so many of us have trouble leaving pain behind is our tendency to think, "That shouldn't have happened to me. That was unfair." When we allow such thinking to dominate our thoughts, we begin to harbor resentments.

Some years ago, *Fortune* magazine conducted a survey of many of the chief executive officers of Fortune 500 companies. The goal was to try to find traits that these successful people had in common. Surprising to say, there weren't many! Some of these top executives had gone to excellent universities, others not. Some brought years of experience to their jobs, while others had enjoyed a quicker rise to success. One of the few things they shared was that, along the way, they had each experienced a major career setback. Most of them, in fact, had been *fired* from at least one job. Understandably, many at the time felt they had been treated unfairly.

Dwelling on life's unfairness and cruelties will not make your life better. Those CEOs learned to move beyond setbacks. We might even conclude that, without confrontation with negative events, they would not be where they are today.

There are many other examples of this process of continual self-rejuvenation:

- *I recall that on occasion Dr. Norman Vincent Peale would give a sermon that fell short of his usual standards. When that happened, he would comment to me, "The best thing I have going for me is next Sunday." I never knew him to dwell on a past failure.*

- *The famous opera singer Jerome Hines, who has been "written off" by the critics time and time again as someone whose career is over, just keeps on singing successfully, well past the age of seventy. Just last year, he was praised by a major critic for a "phenomenal" performance in Boston. The secret of his success? He flatly states, "Every time I get knocked down, I just get back up again."*

- *I also recall the famous story about Babe Ruth—repeated so often it has nearly become a cliché. It is simply that in order to become a great home-run hitter, he also had to strike out more often than anyone else. A cliché perhaps, but it does add statistical heft to the principle that we can either dwell on life's setbacks or know our potential and turn our attention forward to the next opportunity.*

Several years ago I saw a televised interview with Steve Palermo, formerly an umpire in professional baseball. One night, after a game in Dallas, he stopped at a convenience store with some friends. A hold-up occurred, and as Steve chased after the thieves, one of them turned and shot him. Steve was paralyzed. The doctors told him he would probably never walk again. Yet since there was a little feeling in his legs, Steve went beyond the prescribed routine of physical therapy and finally, he was able to walk at least a little. Steve told the interviewer, "You can have all the CAT scans and MRIs in the world that can get accurate images of a man's insides, but until you can take a picture of a man's spirit, you can't tell him that he can't walk."

Consider a child who is just learning to walk. That child falls down. Gets up. Falls down again. And again gets up. You would think that any child in his or her right mind would get discouraged and give up. But children are indomitable.

That is a capability which is built into the human psyche. We are made to try again.

Somewhere in you is the "get-up-again" spirit you had as a child. That is your spirit. Your main task in life is to reclaim it.

Become a "Today Bloomer"

There have been times when I wished my life had been a meteoric success—one of those stories of a youngster who finds his or her talent and scores a stunning success before reaching the age of thirty—or at least by age forty.

We've all known people who have done that—brilliant prodigies who are famous musicians while still in their teens, or twenty-five-year-old authors whose books make the best-seller list, or youthful actresses whose pictures suddenly appear on the covers of every major magazine.

I am grateful I did not experience early success. It would have been dangerous because it would have been empty and absent of the hard work of processing each struggling moment of personal growth. Each, an essential experience.

I have seen too many people suffer from getting too much too soon. Such early successes often suffer for a time under a distorted idea of how life and growth work.

I consider myself a late bloomer. Late bloomers, I believe, have it best. And hopefully, I am still blooming.

To start with, I was not a good student. I was not disciplined. But fortunately, I had just enough native intelligence to pass the tests and write the papers to get by. And I just got by.

I realize today I feel badly about that. I cheated myself by taking the easy way too many times and by not doing my very best from my earliest days. Yet the fact that I did those things did not mean that I had ruined my chances of coming into my own. I just had to do a lot of catching up and compensating for the things I missed as a student.

Progress for me began when I found my niche. From then on, I didn't look back. Yes, I still find myself experiencing a tinge of insecurity. I feel it when I look out into the congregation and see so many intelligent, even influential, people sitting there—especially former teachers or students who excelled with their studies. An inner voice of doubt can tell me, "Arthur, do you really have anything of value to say to these people?"

I know those fears are rooted in old, limiting self-beliefs that stem from my earliest years, when I was barely making the grade. Yet I also know that I could have allowed those self-doubts to become my self-definition. That would have been a counterproductive attitude, and I would have gotten stuck.

Don't we all know people who are obviously gifted, talented, and capable of great things, yet who are hobbled by self-doubts that keep them back?

Please know that growth must be forever and that it is possible for you, at whatever age, to grow up and become the person you know deep down you are capable of being. I'd urge you to take a look at limiting self-beliefs, too. No matter how young you are, you have the option of blooming today.

Forgive Someone

I had a conversation recently with a friend who happens to be an eighty-two-year-old woman. As we discussed her life and the many important issues she is facing at this time of her life, she mentioned that she felt incapacitated in life because of her childhood.

I inquired as gently as I could, and she told me that she still felt injured because of her relationship with her mother. Even at the advanced age of eighty-two, she is still unable to forgive that long-dead parent for certain things—things the woman viewed as "unpardonable."

We agreed that, at her age, it was probably time to get past these problems, so I suggested gently, "Why don't you forgive your mother?" I was not prepared for the emotional reaction triggered by that simple suggestion. She replied that she was just not able to forgive her mother—that the harm she had suffered was simply too great. And I saw that her inability to forgive was continuing to do her harm, even into her eighties.

It is amazing what we carry with us, even into old age! And it is amazing how much of life we lose because we don't do the work of forgiving.

Perhaps by making the simple suggestion, "Forgive your mother," I had been insensitive and naive. But unless we deal with our need to forgive, we stay mired in hurts and resentments. This is a sad human phenomenon.

It is never easy to forgive someone. It requires a lot of emotional work, and it takes time for a major hurt. But it is work that must be done if we are to grow.

Personally, I have been surprised at times at my inability to quickly and easily forgive. Though my mind will say I must forgive, my emotions are not as eager. The act of forgiving seems to demand time and enormous inner work.

Like many people, I have been seduced by the lure of blame. Like many people, I found it easier to point a finger at someone else instead of taking responsibility for solving my problems myself.

After all, "It's her fault" or "It's his fault" can be very seductive excuses for not doing the work we must do. Yet isn't settling up on such counts an essential part of moving on? When we are injured, it is our responsibility—to ourselves and to others—to begin the process of forgiving.

I know that this is not easy advice to follow. I have observed that forgiveness for the big hurts is rare. People are sometimes so injured that they don't want to do the work or to give the benefit of the doubt to another person. Or sometimes, they simply don't know that they have the option to do the work of forgiving.

I frequently remind myself of a conversation about forgiveness, between Jesus and his disciple Peter. Scripture reports that Peter asked, "How many times should I forgive? Seven times?" And Jesus' response was, "No, you must forgive seven times seventy times."

Jesus was not being quantitative here, saying that we should keep count. He was telling Peter that forgiveness is more a state of mind than any finite activity. We need to be predisposed toward forgiveness. When confronted with a hurt, we need to press on until we forgive and are released from its imprisonment and resentment.

Make Forgiveness a Regular Practice

I'm impressed by one lesson about forgiveness that is told by Dr. Doris Donnelly in her wonderful book, *Learning to Forgive.* She relates that, according to one law of the Talmud, if you are given the choice of first helping a friend or helping an enemy, you should help the enemy first.

Why? According to the Talmud, when you help an enemy, you destroy first the hostile emotions and hatred in the enemy, and then in yourself. Instead of an enemy, you have a friend and ally—and so you gain more by helping an enemy than by helping a friend.

Now, forgiving your enemies can be difficult. Yet here's a simple process that can help you get started letting go of emotions that can only be detrimental to you.

I'd urge you to take a few minutes to identify people who you blame and to begin the process of getting past it. There is no easy out here—you have to do some difficult emotional work and confront some negative feelings.

Here are some steps to take:

Pray for the person you need to forgive. We know that Jesus said, "Love your neighbor, even when your neighbor is unfriendly . . . . Pray for the person who tries to harm you."

You may be reacting to this advice by thinking, "Pray for the people who have done me harm? No way! I can't!"

What negative feelings this step can conjure up! Yet it is often essential in the forgiveness process. Many years ago I had to dismiss a member of the church staff. In the days following, this person spread malicious rumors about me and other people in the church, creating enormous turmoil and unrest. I was deeply hurt and angry. I wanted to lash out at him, announcing to the world the irresponsible and reckless work of his tongue. But I was forced to put into practice that which I had preached about so many times. Forgive him.

I had no idea how difficult it would be and how long it would take. For two solid years, I prayed for him every day. I prayed good things for him, even though I didn't feel loving thoughts. I asked God to bless him. I prayed that he might prosper. I felt I had to do this because I didn't like to live with myself while I was having such mean-spirited thoughts about another human being.

And one day, two years after he left, I had a remarkable experience in prayer. I suddenly realized that I no longer had to pray for this man. An inner voice was saying, "You don't need to pray for him any more." And from that day on, my feelings changed and anger was gone. I was released from the prison of regret and hurtful feelings.

Now, did I forgive that man myself? In a way I can say so. But in reality, it wasn't me. I did not act alone. In fact, I don't believe human beings, acting on their own, can forgive others for some really major hurts. We need the help of a higher power to finally relieve us from the bondage of our unforgiving hearts.

Take personal responsibility for the harm the "unforgivable" person has caused. Another difficult step, to be sure! After all, pride is the greatest obstacle to forgiveness. Yet if you blame a business partner for bad decisions that cost you a business, for example, you are really shifting the weight of responsibility away from yourself. That is pride at work. Or if you blame a former spouse for causing emotional pain or costing you important years of your life, you're ducking responsibility for your own healing. In many instances where we direct blame at another person, we are simply looking for an out that lets us divert blame from ourselves. If we can set pride and ego aside and directly face ourselves—possibly even seeing the part we might have played that contributed to the problem—we discover tools we need to do even better in the future.

By accepting responsibility for a failed business or a failed marriage, for instance, we can often begin to analyze negative patterns in ourselves and understand how to avoid them in the future. We empower ourselves to learn by saying, "Here's the mistake I made . . . . Here's how I can avoid making it a second time."

Actively forgive the person you blame. Here is another opportunity to create a dividing line between today and the past. You can conjure up an image of the person you blame and say, "I forgive you." The results of this simple step can be surprisingly emotional and liberating. You are on your way to complete forgiveness.

When you also pray for someone, you will find that part of the emotional weight you're carrying lifts from your shoulders. You begin to live better, today.

Tell the offending person, "I forgive you." Now, here you may be thinking that I've gone too far. Yet I'd urge you to at least consider taking this step as part of the liberating process of forgiveness. Interestingly, the teachings of the Torah are quite clear on this as part of the act of forgiveness that accompanies the start of each Jewish New Year. If you are forgiving someone, you are expected to actually tell that person, "I forgive you."

That can be tough. Sometimes the harm someone did to you is simply so extreme that you cannot even consider this step. Yet we have all seen people who have assumed this kind of stance toward aggressors—the crime victims who forgive the people who did harm to them or their families, for instance. For Christians, doing so means adhering to some of the teachings of Christ that are among the very most difficult to follow.

Yet I also know that it is possible to actively forgive people—even those who are no longer alive. In his book, *Where Do I Go From Here?*, Dr. Kenneth Ruge tells this story about a woman who placed a call to one of the crisis intervention lines at Marble Collegiate Church:

> *A woman called to say that she was hearing the voice of her dead father. My first thought was that this woman probably needed medication and a good therapist. As she continued her story, however, it became evident that more was at work here. She explained that the voice she was hearing was not her father's actual voice. She kept hearing the same criticism, . . . words that her father used to direct at her. Her father had been dead for three years, but she continued to have ambivalent feelings about him. I suggested that she go visit him at the cemetery, go with a trusted friend or relative and have a conversation with him, bringing up these critical patterns. I suggested she have this encounter in a loving way that affirmed her father's positive parenting contribution.*
>
> *One week later she called to tell me that she had visited the cemetery with her sister. They had had a conversation with her father about his criticisms, explaining that they wanted to let go of the patterns they had learned. In a creative gesture, she left a note expressing her love for her father and a rose. In the weeks that*

followed, she experienced a significant reduction of internal criticism. The visit to the cemetery seemed to have "melted" or discharged the power of the paternal disapproval.

I will never say that forgiveness is easy. It isn't. Of all the simple steps we take together in these pages, it may be the most challenging. It is simple to understand, yet emotionally challenging and even taxing to carry out.

Yet forgiving can be a call to greatness, to an extraordinary life, to a life that is distinguished. Think about the great people of the world—in your own life and in history. You'll soon see that one of the keys to leading an exceptional life is learning to forgive.

Make Peace with Your Tragedy

We've been sharing ideas and insights on letting go of life's unfortunate experiences—the frictions we felt with parents, the personal setbacks, the self-doubts and ill feelings we harbor toward others.

At this point, I'd like to suggest you take an even greater step—or, at least, that you begin working on it. I'd like you to take a look at the tragedies in your life and to start doing the work you need to break the hold they exert on the life you are leading today.

Who hasn't experienced a tragedy? No one is immune from them.

After all, tragedy is not unusual. It is a given probability of life.

Hard as it is to accept, tragedy is actually an expected and predictable part of life. Tragedy does not mean you or anyone is being singled out or victimized, even though you may sometimes feel that way.

There are certain givens that go along with being human. We are born in a certain place, to certain parents at a particular time, and with particular genes. Sometimes, we experience tragedy in our early years—the premature death of a parent or a sibling. Or sometimes, through a disease or injury. Sometimes, we are blessedly immune from tragedy until later in our lives, then find ourselves nearly destroyed when a marriage dissolves or some other personal cataclysm unsettles our expectations about what the world "is supposed to be about."

Consider these words from a young man I know:

Up until the age of twenty-one, I actually believed no one I knew was ever going to die. Then, in the course of twenty-four hours, I learned otherwise. I was with my father when he had his heart attack. I rode with him in an ambulance to a hospital. I sat with him in intensive care. I kissed him goodbye when he went into surgery. I sat in a waiting room and waited to hear that he had died.

But even in the midst of it I did not see these horrific events as unusual. Somewhere inside me, a voice seemed to be saying, "This is another part of life." And somehow, despite it all, I remained calm.

Inevitably, tragic things happen. It's part of the human experience. Yet some of us remain mired in tragedy, allowing its misfortune to untrack us, effectively destroying our lives. Others are able to put it in perspective, loosen its immobilizing force, and move on. With the right kind of outlook, we empower ourselves to avoid the bitterness that can set in and color our lives.

For some of us, tragedies open important doors of personal change and growth. The other day, I walked with my dear friend Paula D'Arcy, one of the most effective writers, speakers, and counselors in dealing with tragedies and the grief that follows. Her tragedy was the loss of her husband and three-year-old daughter in an automobile accident. Facing the loss and its profound pain caused her to look for faith. It opened the doors to an incredible spiritual journey, through which her pain has served to help others overcome their own pain.

I asked her if any, or even some, of this spiritual growth would have happened without the accident. She pondered a moment and said, "Probably not."

Continuing to grow despite such profound tragedy cannot be easy. I am keenly aware of that fact. Yet the results can be worth the hard work required. Along with the negative repercussions of a tragic event, there are good results, too. The fabric of our lives can become stronger and more beautiful as we become enriched with a stronger character, a wiser mind, and even a more beautiful soul.

One of my favorite passages from the New Testament is of St. Paul's letter to the Philippians. St. Paul's life seemingly was one in which one tragedy followed another. His was a tough journey. And yet he was inspired, by his experience, to say that through his faith in God, "All things work together for good."

He believed that, with God's help, any misfortunes, losses, and tragedies could sometimes build something good. Having hope for a better day is an essential ingredient in moving past a tragedy.

Hope may seem illogical, irrational, and nonsensical. Yet it truly is a tender thread that carries us across the deepest abysses of life.

The entire message of Judeo-Christian thinking is that the worst things can happen but we still arrive at a better place. The Jews could languish in slavery and be saved. A crucifixion, which is as terrible as anything that can happen to a human, can lead to something extraordinary. Out of darkness comes light. Out of tragedy comes joy.

We've all had tragedies. The work you need to do on yours will not be simple. Yet there comes a critical moment when we each make a decision to either orient ourselves toward the light of hope or the darkness of despair.

It's hard work, but it is a decision you can make—to use the ingredients of your tragedy to mold a stronger and fuller life. You can choose to be a victor, not a victim.

CHAPTER SIX

Banish Prejudice from Your Life

I cannot think of one benefit of prejudice. When it is allowed to exist unchallenged in our hearts, it works as a powerful evil that causes us to blindly miss —and dismiss—the spirits and souls of countless other human beings.

In prejudice, we forget our own humanity. We live diminished lives.

In the Christian faith, Jesus offers a powerful example for freeing oneself from prejudice. He experienced the pain of hatred and prejudice, and yet he said, "Judge not" and "Love one another." He put this great truth in simple, straightforward language.

The instruction not to hate lies at the heart of all great religions. Whatever your faith or belief system, you can find within it words of similar high-mindedness and kindness. When we accept the responsibility that it is our job to love other people, we open the door to a better way of living.

Love and hate cannot coexist.

If you are to live life fully, as a caring human being, you must strive to love all people. Essentially, it all boils down to a choice, the choice to love. Or the choice to hate.

Choose love.

Don't Pass Hatred Along

I have always been appalled, and still am shocked, by the dislikes, prejudices, and hatreds people have for others because they're of a different religion, race, nationality, or sexual orientation. Because of any kind of difference.

I am appalled I think because, when I was a child, I was aware that my parents had immigrated here from another country. We felt that one great thing about life in America was that many people, with many differences, had come together to make a great country.

In my family, we were very conscious of those differences, it is true. We were different from some other people, and other people were different from us. That was part of being American. And oh, how wonderful it was to be here! I have always been fascinated by, and drawn to, cultures and races and religions that were different from my own.

Although we lived in a very small city, our home was in a very diverse part of town. There were Protestants, Catholics, and Jews. There were some African-Americans and Syrians, Armenians, Italians, English, Germans, French-Canadians, Irish, and Greeks. Quite a mix of people for a small city.

Somehow, it was natural and good to be different, and I was always fascinated by differences.

But then I became aware of some of the undercurrents of prejudice that ran through this wonderful society. Why were people prejudiced here in America, when most people had arrived on these shores to overcome prejudice—or, as in the case of African-Americans, had arrived as a direct result of slavery, which is a level of prejudice that seems unthinkable today? Why ever go back to hating? America was a place to make a fresh start.

I still remember one of the first times I witnessed prejudice. I was in the third grade, and I was shocked by it. It was almost Thanksgiving, and our class was given lessons about the gestures of friendship that Native Americans made toward early European settlers. That was a point of the holiday. Yet seemingly in the next breath, I witnessed prejudice against the one Native American in our school, a girl who was in my class. I personally was so impressed and excited that we had a true Native American in my class. But then I became aware that there were other kids who were making fun of her. It just didn't compute.

Then, I remember another hard lesson I learned—again, in school. I was eight years old when World War II began—on December 7, 1941. The next day, my teacher was decorating our class Christmas tree. She was standing on a ladder, putting on the star at the top. Suddenly, she looked at the star, and she said, "Oh, this is from Japan. I can't use it." And she crumpled up that symbol of Christmas, tossed it into a wastepaper basket, and made a pejorative remark about the Japanese.

Even at eight years of age, I wondered why an entire people should be condemned because of the actions of some individuals who happened to be of their nationality.

Again, I was brought face to face with prejudice.

Some years later, when I left the security of my home environment and went off to college, I experienced prejudice myself, as a victim. A few weeks before the Christmas holiday, I started dating a young woman whom I liked, and who liked me. We got along beautifully. After vacation, excited about seeing her again, I called her for a date. But she abruptly told me that she could not see me or speak to me any more. And after that, she literally would not *talk* to me. I was devastated.

Unable to learn from her why she rejected me, I sought the answer from her roommate, who eventually told me that my friend's parents had found out I am of Italian heritage, and they had forbidden her to date me or even to speak to me. I remember thinking that they disliked me without even knowing me. And I remember how painful that was. I would have felt differently if they had disliked me for something I had done. But this was blanket prejudice, and I couldn't fight it.

I got a sense of what it feels like to be disliked and cut off simply because of my heritage.

One of the sad mysteries of life for me is why people, in order to feel superior, look down on others. And to complicate things further, many people who are victims of prejudice themselves fight hate with equal amounts of hatred that they direct at others.

Prejudice begets prejudice. Hate begets hate.

Don't let that happen in *your* life. Chances are you've encountered prejudice. In one way or another, we all have. And we have felt prejudice directed against us.

Yet you have a choice to make. You can either pass hate along, or you can decide, "Hate stops here."

It takes work and discipline to take the higher road on this issue—a certain "setting aside" of your ego. But you can do it. The first step is to decide it's the right thing to do.

Helpful to me in dealing with my temptations to direct prejudice against others is a song I learned in Sunday School. Its simple, heartfelt message has probably done more to shape my attitude toward others—especially toward those who are different from me—than nearly anything else:

> *Jesus loves the little children,*
> *All the children of the world,*
> *Red and yellow, black and white,*
> *All are precious in His sight.*
> *Jesus loves the little children of the world.*

Try to Live One Day
without Prejudice

When we hear the word "love," we generally think of romantic love—a love that's sweet, sentimental, and tender. Romantic love is wonderful. We give it our all, our very best, when we have the opportunity to do so.

When we are in love, we see the best in that other person. We notice everything good. We listen with deep interest when they speak. We find ourselves adjusting to new ways of thinking and new outlooks on the world.

If you can live for just one day with that kind of love for everyone, I know you will see your life transformed.

Wouldn't that be a wonderful day, one in which we could feel the joy of experiencing only tender, caring, and warm regard toward all people? We might return home exhausted, but what a transforming experience it would be.

Where is it written that we can't live like that? Well, perhaps we can. I believe the ability to do so is in us—if we start small, by doing it for just one day.

What if tomorrow morning you left your house committed to loving everybody with a deep interest, a passion? You'd walk out the door, and you'd feel an active affection for whomever you met—your neighbor, your doorman, the bus driver, the mail carrier. When you went into a store, train, or town, you'd feel an enthusiastic, caring love for all the people there.

When you got to the office, even with all the problems you might encounter, you'd decide that you were going to have a loving feeling for everybody, no matter what. No matter how people treated you. No matter how irritating they might be. No matter what, you'd act in a loving way toward them.

Yet while you are learning to develop a passion for people, you might also discover something very interesting about yourself—something a little uncomfortable, too. You might discover that you find it harder to love some people than others. And that knowledge may lead you to some uncomfortable conclusions about yourself.

After all, the people in question may not be unlovable. The problem may be a pesky little demon that slips into the corners of your consciousness and appeals to your dark side. Perhaps the people you find it harder to love are white, or black, or Asian, or Jewish, or homosexual, or members of some other definable group.

It can be difficult to accept the fact that you are prejudiced, that that demon is part of your outlook and habitual way of dealing with the world.

Yet, difficult opponent though he may be, that little demon is not invincible. Love is astonishing. It holds the power to transform your life from one of divisiveness and hatred to unity and affection. And, most astonishing of all, you don't have to go on loving for weeks or months before your life will be transformed. The major step you take is to live in love for just one day.

Try it. It's something you can do, tomorrow, just as soon as you step out your door. And you'll be surprised by what you will learn, and how it will change your life.

Stick to the Higher, Rockier Road

Starting your personal journey away from prejudice is a revealing, exciting experience. That first day we just explored together—that day without hate—just might be the most important step you take to free yourself from prejudice, because it is the first one.

What a change! It was elating, wasn't it?

But the truth is that we've only begun, and hard work may lie ahead. Major changes rarely come quite so easily.

I like to think of this life change (all major life changes, really) as similar to climbing a mountain. When you begin to climb a mountain, the road is wide at the bottom. You can move along easily, swinging your arms happily, with a new sense of purpose. Your way is not blocked, and you have a good feeling about where you are going. But as you climb, things become a little more difficult and may turn out to be somewhat different than you expected. The road narrows and becomes more challenging. Obstacles appear in your path. And the process of moving ahead becomes more exhausting and frustrating.

But once you make this hard climb, you come to a place where you see a wider, more magnificent panorama of life around you. When you finally get to this narrow road in life, you've made a tough climb, but you've reached a better place. You finally have a broad perspective of the issues you've been working through.

This process is part of living a thoughtful, evolving life. It is in marked contrast to what many people do—sticking to the low, wide easy road by accepting the lowest common denominator.

Sometimes, the road becomes very narrow and very difficult. Let me share a story with you.

Something happened to me during the 1980s that illustrates how prejudice can develop, even in people who are trying to be loving and fair.

I remember the day clearly. It was mid-June, and I had just conducted a funeral at a church in Brooklyn. I was carrying my prayer book, with my robe over my arm. I was walking toward my car on a beautiful sunny day, and I felt safe.

But I was suddenly stopped by three teenage boys. One of them held a knife to my stomach while the others robbed me.

If you have had such an encounter, you know how it feels. And you also know the lingering effects, how the fear hangs on. For months afterward, any time I saw teenage boys about the age and size and dress of those boys who robbed me, I had a visceral reaction. They were my enemies, even though I didn't know them.

I could have reasoned, "I have a right to fear those kids." But I wasn't fearing the boys who had robbed me. I was fearing other people who looked like them—and that's a very different matter indeed.

I knew that the demon prejudice was at work in me.

I had to take on my reaction and work it through, telling myself that not all teenagers who looked like my attackers were evil. It was a process that took time, like walking one of those "narrow roads" to a higher place.

Yet I had to make that journey. Otherwise, I would have allowed my whole internal system to build up a rigid resistance to people I didn't even know.

Take the "higher road." Confront head on the justifications and subterfuges you've erected as obstacles to loving other people:

> *I like everybody, it's just that members of that one particular group have a way of getting under my skin.*

> *Why do they all. . .?*

> *I had a bad experience with one of them once, and I'm not going to let it happen to me again. . .*

> *I'm not prejudiced against African-Americans, or Hispanics, or Japanese or whites or Italians, but there is one other group where I draw the line. . .*

You can get morally "lazy" and allow yourself to get seduced and trapped by this kind of thinking. Or you can stay in charge, and keep growing, challenging though it may be.

Progress in life's tough challenges is rarely easy. When you are tempted by the demon prejudice, you have to remind yourself to stand tall—to take the higher, better road, and to arrive at a better place.

With work, you can become bigger than your prejudice. Inside you is enormous love. You know it's there.

Let it happen.

Draw the Line Nowhere

There's one issue of prejudice I'd like to confront head on.

There is something terrible going on in America and all parts of the world. Many people are being abused, shunned, hated, and even beaten and killed because of their sexual orientation.

I know all too well the internal justifications and defenses we can set up when we decide that we're not prejudiced against most people—but that it's permissible to hate people who are gay. For many years I harbored my own blanket prejudice against them. I was thoughtless about gay people, meaning that I really gave no serious thought to the situations homosexuals were in. I believed that all people we call "gay" had made a moral choice and were behaving unwisely and irresponsibly. I was friendly and kind to them in my outer activities. Yet, I kept my distance from them, and regrettably, I even participated in humor that ridiculed them.

I was wrong. So wrong. But thankfully, a change came over me.

My change started when a man who worked for me—someone I thought I knew very well—told me his real story. He was a man of profound integrity, spirituality, and responsibility, someone I respected. And these were his words:

As a child, I always knew I was different. No matter how hard I tried, I just wasn't interested in girls. My whole childhood, as I look back on it, feels like a patchwork quilt

made up of pain, isolation, fear, despair, and loneliness.
I was an outcast.

Since then, I have heard the same story dozens of times. You may have heard similar stories from people you've known who are homosexual. My friend's simple words changed my whole outlook.

This man was homosexual. He had as much choice in the matter as I had in being born white and Italian and heterosexual. You, perhaps, were born tall, or red-haired, or musical, or possessing any number of other traits. You had no choice in the genes given you at birth. It is my belief that homosexuality is more genetic—that the individual has no choice in the matter.

It pains me when people, especially religious leaders, reject gays and lesbians and treat them as pariahs.

There's an old saying that the Christian army is the only army that shoots its wounded. We must stop doing that. It is unacceptable. It's not the way of Christ, who had enormous compassion and who loved all women and men as sisters and brothers, especially those who were outcast and oppressed.

Can't we do that too?

I urge you to confront, in your heart and mind, that one area of prejudice that you may harbor, that place that you fence off in your mind with the words, "I am not prejudiced against anyone, *except . . . .*"

"Except" is not a word we should feel free to use in such an important part of our lives. Where God's rich bounty of life and love are at issue, there can be no exceptions, no exclusions. All people are invited to dine at that rich table.

Reach Out to Just One Person

So far in this chapter, we've been exploring the wrongness of prejudice against groups and individuals who are different from us.

Now I'd like to ask you to take another vital step forward in the process—to reach out not to a group of people, but to *just one person*. That sounds simpler than reaching out to many people, doesn't it?

Well, you may be in for a surprise because, in reality, it can be harder by far.

Yet if we are truly determined to take the "higher road" and drive prejudice from our hearts, this step is essential.

Sometimes, if we are not willing to take this step voluntarily, life thrusts it upon us. We've all heard stories of just that happening to people we've known. Here's a story to consider, told to me by a young woman:

> *My father hated Puerto Ricans and black people, or so he said. Each night over dinner when I was a child, he'd complain about the Hispanic and black workers he supervised in his job as a foreman at a factory. They stole. They were lazy, they were late, they couldn't be trusted. He wanted to "send them back where they came from"—a place he couldn't name when we pressed him on the issue.*
>
> *Then one day, when my dad was driving home from work, a truck forced his car from the road. His car rolled over and ended up on its roof in a ditch. The first people to arrive were other motorists, who took immedi-*

ate action to pull him from the wreck before fire might erupt. When my father got free of the car, he looked up and saw that he probably owed his life to the efforts of a burly Hispanic man, who then put his coat over my dad and kept him comfortable until help arrived. Later, that man came to see my dad in the hospital, and my dad cried tears of gratitude. In the hospital, my dad's surgeons and attendants were African-Americans, Indians, Pakistanis, and people from Latin America. His eyes were opened. Because my dad would not take this issue on himself, the issue took him on. And the experience changed his life in so many positive ways.

I'm struck by the similarity between this story and one in the Scriptures in which Jesus talked openly about prejudice. One day a young man said to him, "Master, tell me, who is my neighbor?" In answer, Jesus responded with a story about a Jewish man who was accosted, beaten up, robbed, and left by the side of the road to die. Three people passed by. The first two were officials of the temple—upstanding citizens. But they chose not to stop and help.

The third man did stop to help. With compassion, he gave the best of himself.

That man was a Samaritan. In those days, Jews and Samaritans were as prejudiced against each other, and with as much ugliness, as any two groups are today. According to Jewish opinion at the time, Samaritans were untrustworthy, bad people. Samaritans directed equal enmity toward Jews. But this Samaritan put aside prejudice and helped a man in need.

In his final answer to the question, "Who is my neighbor?" Jesus admonished the asker to remember the Samaritan and to "go and do thou likewise." In other words, to be there for anyone and everyone who needs help.

Sometimes, it seems, life-altering encounters do "come looking for" people who will not go looking for them. Sometimes, acts of kindness come from unexpected people, and we are forced to rethink our view of the world.

But is it necessary to wait for a transforming experience to broaden your perspective or provide the growth you need in areas you've been avoiding?

I hope not. Where prejudice is concerned, you can effectively take your thinking to a higher level by serving as the catalyst for such growthful encounters yourself, by reaching out and getting to know someone who is a member of a group for which you harbor a dislike.

Connecting with someone as an individual can be a life-transforming event that broadens your perspective and helps drive prejudice away. Let me share a story with you about someone who overcame a deep personal prejudice in just this way.

For a time, I had the habit of stopping at the same coffee shop on many days for a quick breakfast or lunch. In case you might not know, coffee shops are one of the best things about New York. People who become "regulars" really get to know each other. At this particular shop, I got to know one of the waitresses who worked there. I realized she was a spiritually oriented, caring person when I overheard her say to a customer, "I will pray for you."

When she learned I was a minister, we started to chat about some of her issues of faith. She told me she was about to join a new church and said she was really looking forward to it.

Some weeks later, she happened to be waiting on a table where I was having lunch, and I said to her, "When we last talked, you said you were about to join a new church. How did it work out?"

"Yes, I joined that church," she answered. She then hesitated and added, "but then I had to quit."

I was very surprised. I knew she was really looking forward to becoming involved in a new spiritual community.

"Why?" I asked.

"I discovered that the choir director is a homosexual," she answered.

Since the decision to leave was obviously still causing her emotional distress, I asked her to join me at my table for a few minutes. I quickly told her about my own struggles to rid my life of prejudice against homosexuals.

I explained that, by really listening to a gay man, I had overcome my prejudice.

I told her that that man had been an employee of mine for many years. He was honest as the sunshine, respected by everyone, and a very spiritual person. I also explained that I had not known that he was homosexual until he told me his own story, which was one of struggle and survival. As a child, he had no interest in girls. His father, a famous athletic coach, was not approachable on the issue of his son's sexual orientation. Alienated and depressed, the boy grew up to become an alcoholic adult. He finally came to accept himself and live happily and fully, but only after much hard work and suffering. And it was all no fault of his own.

Then I said, "Please sit down with that choir director. Share something about yourself. Then please ask him to tell you his story. Just ask what his life has been like. Get to know the person. Then, if you decide to leave the church, you will be doing it for the right reasons."

When I next saw her, she was obviously glad to see me, and eager to share some news. She said, "You know, I rejoined the church. I even joined the choir."

She had followed my suggestion. She and the choir director got together and talked. She really listened. And she discovered a very special and wonderful human being.

"I know now that people cannot be placed into categories," she told me.

In my opinion, that young woman had tremendous moral courage. Not all of us would have the integrity to sit down with our "enemies." Not all of us would listen carefully and take in what we heard. But she did. And as a result, she grew.

It's a simple step, to reach out to "someone on the other side"—someone you don't expect to like. Yet you can. Simply share your story, and listen.

You don't have to become a close friend to every person who enters into your life—yet you can live with expectation that each new person you meet might become a lasting, valuable friend.

Always give people the chance to earn your love—or your dislike. Remember that wonderful yardstick, the Golden Rule, "Do unto others as you would have others do unto you."

As that Golden Rule clearly states, the first step is up to you.

Black versus White in America: Can't We Get Beyond This?

Nobody chooses where they are going to be born or to whom they are going to be born. We choose none of this. It is all given.

We didn't choose to be white or black, or Americans, or Chinese. It's just the way it is. How stupid and limiting it is for us to eliminate from consideration of goodness whole groups of people simply because they are different from us.

As a white person living in America, I have only a limited sense of what it is like to live as an African-American here—to live each day with hundreds of slights, frustrations, and prejudices.

Unless we have lived as African-Americans, we have little idea of what it is like to live with experiences like these every day of our lives:

- *A Muslim sheik recently told me that until ten years ago, most Americans—and virtually all police officers—thought of him as a criminal because he was black and Muslim.*

- *Studies have concluded that taxicabs in our major cities are up to ten times more likely to stop for white Americans than for African-Americans. Even well-dressed black executives—men and women alike—stand by the side of the street as cab after cab passes them by.*

Several years ago, a rabbi I know was visiting an African-American friend who is a professor at Harvard University. They were riding in the professor's car, a Mercedes, when a police officer stopped him, ordered him out, frisked him abusively, and then let him go. When the rabbi asked his friend what was going on, the professor replied, "This happens all the time. Black people are not supposed to be driving a Mercedes."

This is tragic and shameful, shortsighted and stupid.

We can't cure this societal problem by making a personal decision, within our hearts. But we can decide, within our hearts, to take no part in this national tragedy of racism, which is a blight on our national soul.

Provide an Opportunity

Not long ago, a televised profile on *Sixty Minutes* highlighted the fact that failing to lift people up—to provide them with opportunities—is one of the cruelest and basest things human beings can do to each other.

The story centered on a woman who is a pitcher for minor-league baseball in Minnesota. Since she's the only woman in the league, she's obviously good enough to compete on that level. I was impressed by her poise. She is centered and articulate. Yet every day, she confronts the small-minded prejudices of many of the men who surround her, who catcall at her "Go play with the girls!"

This is but one example of the frustrations and troubles women must face because of ingrained prejudices in our society. Numerous men unbelievably seek to keep women down and "in their place," just because they are female.

I like the thinking of Claire Booth Luce, who said that people should "allow a woman to try any job that has been solely for men. If she can make it, she will make it. If she can't, she will fail. But let her try."

Yet we see that prejudice is again at work here. And the psychology of prejudice is quite simple. In order for some people to feel superior, they put someone else down.

A better alternative is available. Love people, lift them up, and honor them.

Isn't that a far better way to prove your superiority—even excellence?

Greet Your Fellow Voyagers
"Soul to Soul"

Some years ago I was having dinner with a physician friend, who happens to be a very spiritual man. As we talked, I made some comments about "some people" and my difficulty in understanding them and relating to them.

Then my friend made a simple remark on the subject that really stopped me cold, and forever changed the way I look at others:

I see people as souls.

What profound words. I was ready to hear them. I needed to.

Souls, yes, we are all souls. Spiritual beings. Yes, souls.

His words helped me come to a new place in my own thinking about people, and my tendencies to be prejudiced.

Aren't we all souls, first and foremost?

Aren't we all created by the same God, and are we not each as valuable to God as any other person might be? Were we not born into this world with certain predetermined differences—our bodies and a predisposition to certain personality traits? Do we not all have character flaws, behavioral mannerisms that annoy or irritate others? Are not some of us brilliant and others limited in intelligence? Are not some of us greatly gifted, while others of us lack for talent?

We can list many other differences in who we are.

Yet behind everything, beyond personality and appearance, we are souls. Special beings. All equal in God's eyes. And each one precious.

Think about that. Meditate on it. It's a simple concept that can exert a profound benefit on the quality of your life and the lives of everyone around you.

CHAPTER SEVEN

Risk to a Brighter Future

M ention risk, and images come to mind of running out into traffic without looking or bungee jumping off a bridge. Those are careless, foolish risks—not the ones we'll explore in this chapter.

Risk is how we grow. It functions as the pivotal point between who we are now and who we are to become. Any time there is growth or change, it follows risk.

When we move to a new job or tell someone we love them, or get married, or become parents, risk is there. If we're too cautious and ban risk from our lives, we remain stuck in place. We never make progress or evolve.

In fact, risking in the right way is the *safest* thing we can do. It helps us move away from places in our lives where we don't belong and into places where we can live more fully.

In the pages that follow, I'll invite you to join me in taking some risks—the *right* kind—and we'll share the experience of moving our lives further along together.

Risk Being Vulnerable

I'd like to consider with you a particular kind of risk, and a very important one. It's the kind of risk where you open yourself up to other people, exposing your inner thoughts and feelings.

Now, you might wonder, why would you want to take a step like that? Why risk criticism and rejection? I can say only that it's a risk that can repay you with an especially rich—and unpredictable—array of rewards.

How emancipating it can be to lower our defenses—when we, in effect, say, "I'm going to expose myself to rejection. I'll just be who I am and dare to express myself. Of course I'm risking rejection, but I'm going to reveal who I really am—warts and all, darkness and light. All."

I'd like to share an experience with you.

Several years ago, I attended a conference on the West Coast with twenty-six other members of the clergy who had come from major churches and institutions across America. To be truthful, the idea of being with a group of my colleagues was not entirely positive. All were very successful, but most were more conservative than I am. Generally I have been criticized, if not condemned, by many of my colleagues who are of a conservative mind.

A week before the conference, I was asked if I would do the morning devotions on the fourth, and last, morning of the conference. It was to be a ten- to fifteen-minute talk on anything I thought appropriate.

Although I had an idea of what I wanted to talk about, I was sort of casing the attendees during the conference. I was trying to get a sense of who they were. And, of course, I listened to the other devotionals to get a feeling for what would be appropriate.

As I listened to those other devotionals, I found that most people were giving talks much like the ones we had all learned to write as sermons when we were in seminary. I'd characterize that kind of talk as "theologically thoughtful."

Everything was correct in those talks, possibly even put together with the intent of impressing the assembly with some elegant turn of phrase or point of erudition. But I found that no person shared anything of himself in those talks. There was no heart. No spirit.

No one offered any self-revelation that opened up a sense of the individual who stood behind the words. Even in my conversations with others as those days went by, most people seemed to have their defenses up. We were all sharing our successes, recounting how wonderful things were for us, how our churches were growing.

I arrived at a decision. I would do something different. I decided, with no well-defined goal in mind, to address something a little curious. I decided to share a part of my own journey in my devotional talk.

When my morning came, I asked everyone to rearrange the chairs from theater-style into a circle. I said, "This morning, my devotional will be a story of my own pain and brokenness and the healing that followed."

I told them that I had been in denial. I said that I was a classic Type A personality, and that had resulted in a major illness. I revealed how, in the face of that illness, I had lost my faith and my ability to pray. I even told how I had, at the suggestion of my surgeon, started seeing a psychiatrist.

I held nothing back, including the fact that my psychiatrist was helping me get in touch with my feelings, my anger, my control needs—who I was. I told them I was finding the courage to begin to face myself, deep down.

This was a huge risk to take, as I was aware that perhaps ninety percent of the clergy in attendance would see therapy as a sign of weakness—an admission that faith alone could not solve all problems.

About midway through my talk, I became aware that people were not only listening but they seemed riveted to what I was saying. It was clear to me that they were looking at their own personalities, their fears, loneliness, weakness—their vulnerabilities. No one can argue with another person's story.

I had to leave to catch a plane just after my devotional. As I walked from the room, several people walked along with me, each in his own way saying, "You were talking directly to me . . . to all of us. We're not free to say how we really feel."

Was my talk a risky thing to do? Absolutely. Yet it taught me something invaluable, even amazing. We are emancipated when we allow ourselves to share something true and painful about ourselves. When we take this kind of risk, two things happen. We are freed, and the people around us are freed as well.

Where are you in your own journey? Do you need to open up to someone with what you are really feeling, with who you really are? Are you afraid of risking this?

I challenge you to find someone you can trust and with whom you can be open and honest, beginning and continuing the process of being who you really are.

Try it, and the response may change your life. Even more remarkable, it may change other lives, too.

Move Forward with a Brave Heart

It takes courage to become the kind of person you'd like to become. It takes heart to act courageously.

Interesting to note, the word *courage* itself comes from *cor,* the Latin word for heart. When we act with courage, our hearts are empowering us to move ahead. Our actions are heartfelt because when we have courage, we are listening to a vital, inner voice. That inner heartfelt urging voice calls us into action.

If you would like to see courage visibly displayed, I'd urge you to visit Ellis Island in New York Harbor. As you surely know, that small island was the point of arrival for millions of immigrants who came to America to seek new lives. As you enter the main building, you will find displayed remarkable photographs of immigrants just arriving in the New World.

In many of the photographs, you will notice that many people are carrying all their worldly goods in just a suitcase or a trunk. You will see parents with young children.

These are pictures of people who were taking enormous risks. To leave a familiar country behind—family, friends, traditions—to sail to a new country without work or security.

The faces in those photographs tell stories that cannot easily be put into words. All of the immigrants look expectant. Their facial expressions convey hope and courage. In their eyes shines the courage, the determination, the possibility of a new and better life.

My parents were among those who passed through Ellis Island. Seeing those photographs gave me some insight into why my father had a favorite salutation to the people of his small parish in Portland, Maine. Many times I heard him say to a struggling, discouraged person, "Couraggio!"

Couraggio he would say—courage to you!

All of us who reside in the New World are heirs to this rich legacy of courage. Risk is part of the rich tapestry of America. That kind of courage is part of our lives.

America, where you live, is a land of strivers. So I think risking, and courage, are things we should all share.

Don't Let Fear Stall Your Life

We all have the potential to keep growing for as long as we live. Yet all too often, we stay stuck. We make apologies, offer excuses, and make no progress. What keeps us from moving ahead to reach our desires?

Usually, simple fear is at the heart of it. As long as fear is allowed to dominate our lives, we don't move forward.

Fear is not always manifested in sweaty palms, tears, trembling, or other signs of heightened emotions. More often, it exerts its crippling force quietly, in ways that are harder to discern.

Fear is at work when we tell ourselves things like these:

I can't make that career change I'd love to because we couldn't afford it.

I can't tell my children how much I really love them because that would be out of character.

I can't travel abroad because I'm too old and I wouldn't want to become ill in a foreign country.

I'd never get that job because I don't have the qualifications.

There's no point in writing a novel because it wouldn't get published.

Please notice that all those sentences contain the word "because." That word can be one of the greatest, most crippling inhibitors any of us face in our lives.

Please take a moment to consider where that word may be exerting its numbing, immobilizing force to keep you from moving toward what you want to achieve most in your life—toward living your heart's desire.

Let me share with you this story of someone who had learned to move her life forward by banishing fear from the way she chose to lead her life.

Amelia, long one of my dearest friends and a cherished member of the congregation at Marble Collegiate Church, achieved the remarkable life span of one hundred and five years. She was a bright, alert, witty, aware, high-energy woman. She volunteered at the church's seniors' groups, regularly had lunch or dinner with friends, was incessantly on the phone with friends and family—often giving much-sought-after counsel. I was privileged to get to know her when she was eighty-nine.

From the time she was ninety, I would take Amelia to lunch on or around her birthday. When she was ninety-nine I, not knowing if she would live to be one hundred, decided to ask the "big" question that is usually reserved for people who reach the age of one hundred. I asked, "To what do you attribute your longevity?"

The usual answers we hear to that question are, "I didn't drink," "I didn't carry on," "I minded my own business," and the like. I had no idea what this spunky little ninety-nine-year-old would say.

What she said was profound. It caused me to sit up and take notice:

I have learned how not to be afraid.

Wow! What a statement. I realized—Yes, this woman is fearless!

Now, she had been through a lot, especially in her later years. She had been mugged twice. She had broken her hip. She had been widowed, and she had buried two of her three children. She had even been hit by a car! Yet she somehow realized that the only way to keep her active, involved life was to keep vital, even risking new experiences. She could have stayed at home, more justified than most of us to hide behind all the "becauses." Yet she saw that the most detrimental path was to hide away at home, not to keep on moving out into the world despite the risks.

Amelia was a heroine. She was afraid of nothing.

There's another story of a woman who didn't let all the "becauses" keep her stuck in place. Her name is Terrie Williams, head of a large public relations firm in New York City. Ms. Williams's story is a remarkable one. Although she had a background in social work, she nonetheless decided to pursue her "heart's desire" by starting her own public relations firm.

"I had no background or company at the time, but I found a way to approach Eddie Murphy and Miles Davis. I told them, 'I want to do your public relations.' And they were my first two clients."

Interestingly, Ms. Williams's refusal to be stymied by daunting obstacles has allowed her to become one of the most-awarded individuals in public relations today. Her reason? She says that when she feels "butterflies" in her stomach, she knows she is taking the right amount of risk in her life, not staying on safe, familiar ground.

"When I'm sitting in an outer room before a meeting, thinking I must be crazy to try something, that there is no reason the deal I'm suggesting will ever work, then I know I'm taking my life in the right direction."

So the message is clear. You can hide behind your personal "becauses" or become more comfortable with the risks that can move your life forward.

Jump into the Pool

All major religions contain parables and teachings that attest to risk's power to transform lives. There are, of course, many parables in the Bible that attest to it. One of my favorites is the story of the pool at Bethesda. (This pool, incidentally, really existed. It has recently been discovered and excavated in Jerusalem.) It was believed at the time that when the water stirred, an angel was causing it to move. That movement was an indication that the angel was lending healing powers to the water and the first person to jump in would be healed.

People would sit and wait until the water stirred, then seek to be the first one in. The Scriptures relate that one day, Jesus passed by the pool and spoke with a man who had been there for thirty-eight years. When the man was asked why he had not been in the pool first at some point, he replied, "Well, nobody put me in the water. Nobody helped me."

Now, if this man had really wanted help, he would have endeared himself to someone who would have helped him. What probably happened is that after several weeks or months of frustration and disappointment, he took on a "poor-me" attitude and lived in a state of self-pity.

Jesus approached and challenged him with the question, "Do you want to be well?" The man said, "Yes." So Jesus said, "Stand up and walk." Which the man did. But it was a decision that the man made for himself—in effect, to think differently about himself.

This story can be interpreted many ways. But at its most elemental level, it is a story about building an attitude that welcomes risk. It teaches us that we have the ability to choose the mindset that will cause us to be healed or reach other goals we strive for in life. We do not have to sit idly by—certainly, not for thirty-eight years!

Taking that first step is completely and totally up to us. The old phrase, "Come on in, the water's fine!" comes to mind. If you're holding back, why not take that important jump? The water may not be just the right temperature at first since change is uncomfortable at first. But in just a little time, it will feel very much to your liking—even terrific.

Take a Spiritual Risk

As we've discovered together in this chapter, risk may not really be so risky after all.

Instead of danger, it embodies the principles of expansion, enrichment, and inclusion. Through risk, a life becomes bigger, more interesting—and more inclusive of other people.

As you expand your life through risk in this way, I urge you to invite one additional presence into it, too. That presence is the divine—something you might choose to call God, the eternal, a higher power, the spiritual, the infinite. The words you use are very much up to you, and the rewards are certain.

What I'm suggesting here is that you do something very specific, and very special, in conjunction with that divine presence. I'm suggesting that you simply open up an area of your life to the divine—preferably, an area you have never opened up to divine intervention before.

I'm suggesting that you take a very particular kind of risk —a spiritual risk.

How can you do it? I'd like to share some stories that hold at least some of the clues:

I was on my way back from visiting my mother in a hospital where she lay terminally ill," a man states. *"And I didn't know how to bear all the burdens that lay upon me—the financial burdens, the stresses on my family and my work. Life seemed too much for me at that moment. Then as I drove over the crest of one hill, I was suddenly greeted by a wonderful, brilliant orange sun-*

set, and I did something I had never done before. I said aloud, 'God, please help me through this. I can't manage alone.' From that instant onward, the problems didn't disappear. But I somehow felt that my burdens were dramatically reduced. I had established a partnership with something greater than myself."

Or consider this story:

"I didn't know how to talk to my daughter about her life," a woman recalls. "Even at the age of thirteen, she was hanging around with the wrong kind of kids. What lay ahead? Drugs? Teenage pregnancy? Failure in school? Worst of all, she had become hypersensitive and difficult to talk with. So, since there was no direct conversation with her, I turned in desperation to some higher power. One day, I found myself simply saying, 'Dear, dear God, what can you do to help my daughter? What can you do to keep these awful things from happening?' I found myself repeating those words more and more often. There was no miraculous turnaround, at least not at first. But suddenly, six months down the road, I realized that the situation was far better and that I could actually talk to my daughter more. Perhaps it was because my prayers were answered. Perhaps it was because I simply felt calmer and more in control of my own emotions about the problem—and my daughter responded positively to the fact that I was calm, not frantic. I don't know exactly how it happened, but I asked for help, and help came."

In this woman's words lies the essence of what it means to take a spiritual risk. Instead of waiting silently and passively for the problems in your life to recede, you take the risk of asking for help. For many of us—especially the most self-reliant among us, who like to "go it alone"—asking for divine intercession can be a very real risk indeed. It can cause us to reevaluate many things: our beliefs about ourselves, about the world, about God.

Yet isn't that what risk is all about—about pushing back borders and trying things in new ways?

If you haven't yet, I urge you to take a simple step. Take just one problem that's troubling you—the bigger and more sensitive the problem, the better. When you have a moment, ask God about it—or ask the divine, or the spiritual, or whatever presence you prefer.

Take that little risk and ask. And don't be surprised if your life becomes far, far better.

CHAPTER EIGHT

Connect with a Higher Power

I n this chapter, I urge you to connect with something powerful that is within you. It's a powerful resource that is within each of us—something that stands ready to partner with you and lift your life to extraordinary new levels.

This resource is called *prayer* by many people. I am sensitive to the fact that many people have a hard time with that word—either because they have tried to pray and found it difficult, or because their own backgrounds cause them to feel uncomfortable with the concept.

Yet prayer—or a similar process called by another name—brings remarkable changes in life. So as you start this chapter, I ask you to keep an open mind for a while and experiment a little with something new, by taking two preliminary steps.

First, try to set aside preconceptions you may have about prayer, and simply try a few new ideas. If they don't work out for you, we will still be friends, and we will still share further explorations. You can decide that the experiment didn't work for you, you will have lost nothing—and you may be surprised to learn you gained far more than you expected.

Second, if the word *prayer* triggers negative thoughts in you, simply replace that word for a time with other words that seem more comfortable. Try *meditation, reflection*, or even *connecting with a higher power*. Find words that make you comfortable.

The experiment is worth a try.

Tennyson, that deep, deep thinker, said people can solve more problems through prayer than through any other means. And my own experiences and observations confirm it. People who connect with something bigger than themselves often transform their lives.

My own life in prayer has been anything but easy, but I now know that connecting with a higher power really works. It has changed my life, and I have seen it change other lives in countless, remarkable ways.

I urge you to just try. And don't be too surprised if remarkable things begin to happen.

Welcome the Inner,
Higher Power within You

Well into my adult years, I continued to hold to the idea that God was "up there" or "out there" somewhere. To reach that universal being required striving, trying, climbing out of myself. I sensed frustration, even anger. It seemed all but impossible to me. I could never feel connected for very long.

Yet in retrospect, why shouldn't I have believed that God was very, *very* far away? I heard it in Sunday school. My parents told me it was so. I saw it in religious paintings that depicted God as a man who resided somewhere "up there" in the skies. God was in heaven, and heaven was "up there."

I even heard it in the words of the most beloved of all prayers: "Our Father, who art in heaven."

In my classes as a student and readings and conversations, I also encountered the concept that God resides *within* each of us—within you and me. I became aware of Jesus' reference to the Kingdom of God within. Yet I held that view only intellectually. It seemed like a secondary consideration, and it never occurred to me to seek a more intimate connection with God.

So I kept on talking, for years, to a remote God. It was an enormous and frustrating struggle for me. I'd pray for a day or two, sometimes three or four, but I couldn't sustain it. I would stop and then feel enormous guilt. Sometimes, I wondered whether to go on—which would be a pretty cataclysmic decision for a member of the clergy to make, especially to one who really wanted an intimate relationship with God.

Then, on the days when I felt fulfilled in my prayers or saw some positive results, I believed the process was working and I felt more motivated to continue.

I was engaged in a personal experiment with the eternal. Yes, I realized that the results of prayer needed to be claimed with humility and awe, and over years of engaging in the process. Still, my prayer life was bringing me only guilt and remorse. I was engaged in an enormous struggle.

It's interesting that, for me, the biggest breakthrough came because I passed through a time of great personal testing and difficulty. Those were the days that followed the dissolution of my first marriage—truly a hellish time when I lived through a dark night of the soul.

I was filled with pain, loneliness, and depression. I prayed to God, but found that I still didn't fully trust God. My relationship with God was weighing me down and providing no relief or answers.

Only when I really hit bottom did I bump into the reality that an eternal power was fully within, as well as surrounding me.

When I hit bottom, I finally realized that I did not need to reach over the clouds and the mountains to touch the eternal. The eternal was already within me, and at my side, ready to offer me help and the resources I needed to try to piece my life back together.

In those days, I saw that the key is to accept the reality that God is truly within each of us.

God, or the eternal—or whatever you choose to call this powerful, caring presence—is already within us. We don't have to "jump through hoops" to receive grace or benefits.

The only step we need take is to *trust*. Trust in God, then trust and *trust some more*.

The Quaker writer Thomas Kelly said it so well, that inside each individual, deep within the psyche, is a sanctuary. He calls it "the sanctuary of the soul." And so when life's challenges and tensions come upon us, we can go into the inner sanctuary of the soul. There, we will learn to trust that God is within as well as without.

This realization transformed my life. Prayer became not a burden, but a source of joy.

Yes, I am often troubled. I often falter. We all do. Yet my life in the world has become more centered and assured.

I now know that a wonderful power stands ready to lead me safely through the troubled times ahead.

This power stands at your side, too. Stop stretching, straining, and beating yourself up about it. Simply embrace it, for it is there in your mind and heart.

Remember, You Can't Get It Wrong

Some years ago, when a discipline called "Transcendental Meditation" was quickly gaining adherents in the United States, I spoke with a member of my congregation who was trying it out.

"Does it seem to be working for you?" I asked.

"Well, it is really a lot like prayer," she answered. "I was given a simple word called a *mantra* to repeat over and over in my mind."

That concept is not too foreign to me since I have often prayed by repeating the only word I really need to pray, *"God."*

But then she continued to describe her experience in meditation.

"The way meditation is taught has one feature I particularly like. After each of my training sessions, my teacher asked, 'Was meditating that time *easy*?' and, 'Was it *pleasant*?' If some aspect of the way I was meditating didn't fill those criteria, we'd explore a bit to find out why. More often than not, we determined that it wasn't pleasant or easy because I was telling myself, while meditating, that I was doing something incorrectly. The underlying message seemed to be that there was no way to meditate incorrectly. There was only to do it."

In her way, I think this concept mirrors the words of St. Paul, from his Letter to the Romans (Romans 8:26):

Likewise the Spirit helps us in our weakness; for we do not know how to pray as we ought, but the Spirit itself intercedes for us with signs too deep for words.

What St. Paul is telling us here is that we all feel that we don't know how to communicate with a higher power as we ought to. We hesitate to connect because we fear we will do it wrong. But the point is to set aside those concerns and trust—and try anyway. We will not be judged. We will be supported in our efforts.

Perhaps we would all pray more happily, and more often, if we realized that we are not going to be judged on how well we pray. Prayer should be both pleasant and easy—just as easy as a friendly conversation with your best friend or a quiet reflection you share with yourself while enjoying a pleasant walk in the countryside, or a little quiet time alone.

Why, then, is this process of "connecting" different from just a little talk, or that pleasant little walk?

Simply because of the fact that, when you pray, you accept the idea that someone is listening to you. In a simple, comfortable way, you accept that a higher spiritual presence is there with you, sharing your thoughts and conversation.

You might also expect that your efforts might have some kind of positive effect. In that way, praying becomes a way of projecting a thought—making a request or setting an idea before some power that is bigger than yourself.

Beyond those considerations, there is nothing you can do wrong.

With this approach, connecting with the eternal can be a pleasant, joyful part of each day. Over time, it broadens into a profound, limitless well of joy and happiness.

Share the Process
with Someone Else

 Have you thought of praying with someone else? Or if you and another person are trying to solve a problem, have you thought about meditating on that problem together?

Sharing time together, concentrating on a problem or praying about it, is a simple practice that can produce remarkable results. It works with two people. It works with many.

The bottom line is, it works.

Consider these words, spoken by a woman I know whose marriage seemed to have been miraculously healed after years of troubles and friction.

> *We'd tried nearly everything else to solve our problems, and nothing worked. Then one day, we decided to try something different. Instead of identifying problems and talking them through in a therapeutic way, we would simply be quiet together for a few minutes so we could each pray and meditate, hoping for things to get better.*
>
> *Those few quiet minutes, which we then decided to repeat again and again in the months that followed, broke up the log jam of defensiveness and anger between us. Each time we emerged from our shared quiet time, we were able to communicate much more effectively. We seemed to be operating off of the same fundamental, quiet resonance instead of starting from a place of disharmony.*

When we intentionally decide to share a little quiet time together, remarkable things can happen. It may be because, as this woman says, being reflective together frees us to approach problems with a similar, shared mindset and set of emotions. Or quiet time together might be effective because it invites the participation of something "bigger" that intercedes and helps.

When things are not going well in our own efforts, why not get some outside help?

Too often, as Americans, we try to go it alone. We tend to be rugged individualists, forgetting that people need each other. Sharing prayer or meditative time together is one way to break that pattern. And it really gets results.

Pray for Someone Else

Some years ago, a member of my congregation was facing a serious operation. She was given only a fifty-fifty chance of survival. Although I was on vacation on the day she went into the hospital and I was far away, I knew there was something I could do to help.

I sat on the back porch of my cottage during the early morning quiet and I commenced praying for her. I remember the intense focus, the energy of the prayer. And I prayed for a very long time. That period of prayer was, I believe, one of the deepest and most concentrated of my life.

Finally, I arrived at a point where something within said she would survive the surgery. Refreshed and assured, I resumed my day's activities.

Later that day, her husband called to report on the operation. I knew in advance what he would say.

"She made it and will be fine," he said to me.

I thanked him for calling and told him of the assurance that had come earlier in the day during my prayer time.

Praying for someone else is one of the most extraordinary experiences I can think of. It is a way of loving and caring.

One of my favorite prayers is a Quaker prayer called "The Prayer of Beholding." It is one of the most uplifting and healing of all prayers. I pray it often myself and regularly suggest it to my congregation during the prayer time in our worship service.

To pray this prayer, you hold the person you are praying for in the warm and healing glow of God's love. Visualize the person surrounded by this soft and warm light. Project loving thoughts. See the person enveloped in God's perfect love. Then add to the prayer by telling the other of your prayer—that you prayed in this loving way.

The person is twice-blessed! And often the results are in the wondrous realm of the mysterious.

In that moment, you caught a glimpse of the grace that awaits each of us. It was simple, and it really worked.

Accept a Mystery

Many of us love mysteries. We like nothing more than to read a mystery novel or watch a movie. We like to watch as little clues are provided about the final outcome. Then, when the mystery is resolved or the case is solved, we enjoy the moment when we finally say, "Aha! Now I know what has been going on through this story." Or even, "I knew the real outcome all along."

Connecting with a higher power can work in a similar way because often, as part of the process, we receive mysterious ideas, words, phrases, or even directives—commands, if you will. If we are willing to accept these mysterious clues, we can often engage in a remarkable process of self-discovery.

Mysteries do come to us in prayer, mysteries that contain missions and issues that we are to think about and deal with.

I remember a time in my own life when my life seemed to be in good shape. Family, health, job—everything appeared to be balanced. But underneath, I was churning. I knew something was wrong. I was unsettled, unfocused, anxious.

And at times when I felt most unsettled, I found myself uttering different kinds of prayers. I must have experimented with a dozen different prayers in an effort to fix my inner turmoil.

Then, one summer morning, I read the Biblical story of Jesus and a blind man. Jesus asked what he could do to help, and the man answered, enigmatically, "That I might receive my sight."

After I read this passage, I went out for my morning walk. And suddenly, an idea came to me very strongly, really in the form of a command.

I found myself saying, "Arthur, that is your prayer, 'that I might receive my sight.' You are to pray this prayer."

Its meaning was still cloudy for me, but I knew that it was to become my prayer for the foreseeable future. It was a mystery—both puzzling and somehow elating. I began to pray it often, many times a day. I was confident it was right, and I trusted that one day, my inner churning would be settled.

Several months later, some wonderful things happened in my life. I thought, "This is it, my prayer has been answered!" I was elated.

Yet that high was followed in a few days by a more than corresponding low. I found myself facing surgery, at a time when Dr. Norman Vincent Peale had just retired and I was newly in charge at Marble Collegiate Church. I was just beginning my life there after his departure. And then, four weeks after his retirement, I was hospitalized with open-heart surgery.

The timing was terrible! And to tell the truth, I didn't handle it well at first. I was numb. I lost faith in everything. I couldn't pray. I was in a fog. If I were to describe my state with colors, I was dark gray, almost black.

Although I didn't know it at the time, my prayer was being answered. You will recall my earlier story that while I was in the hospital, a surgeon said to me, "Arthur, you know this kind of thing just doesn't happen," meaning my illness wasn't a result of external forces. My internal state had contributed to my sickness.

What did he mean, I needed to know. I listened and took his advice. At his urging, I started to work with a psychiatrist. I began to get in touch with my emotional material. I began the process of addressing many things that were wrong in my life.

I began a long process of learning. The clogged arteries that required bypasses were the symptoms of deeper problems. I needed expert, professional help to get in touch with my issues.

Then one day, I realized all the pain and confusion, the illness and the surgery, were answers to my prayer. The mystery was solved.

My "sight" was a new, deeper level of understanding about myself, my past, and my world. I didn't get to my new level of sight through some "click" or instant cure from above. I had to pass through very tough times and work hard. But in the end, my prayer was answered, my mystery solved.

I'd also like to share with you the good news about the prayer that I live with day and night now. In fact, I think it may have become my prayer for life. I received my impetus to begin praying with it when I was in another dark, difficult period. It seems I do my learning and growing when I am facing hard times.

You know the saying, "When the student is ready, the teacher appears"? It is my life story. During this period I was lonely, depressed and I had lost the essence of my faith. I believed in God, but I didn't trust myself to God for the next five minutes. I was trying to solve all problems in my own way.

Then I came upon a prayer I had known about—a prayer called "The Jesus Prayer." I began to use it, and it has probably become my prayer for life. . .

Lord Jesus Christ, have mercy on me,
make haste to help me, rescue me and save me,
do your will in my life.

That prayer suddenly spoke to me in some deep, resonant way. I did as I learned one must do with this prayer. I prayed it constantly, without ceasing. I began repeating it hundreds and hundreds and thousands and thousands of times. I pray it day after day—in the elevator, when I'm walking, even when I'm in conversation. I discovered it is a way to try to stay open to the movement of a higher power to lead me to where I'm supposed to be going, what I'm supposed to be doing. The last line—*do your will in my life*—is the bottom line of all praying. To submit to divine will.

In a few days I realized my crisis in faith had passed—I was trusting God. And I began to experience a series of coincidences—those mysterious happenings no human can arrange.

My mysterious relationship with this little prayer may have a real, final revelation—one of those "Aha!" moments when I suddenly encounter its deep message for me. Or that message may be revealed to me every day, as I experience the power of this prayer to direct and transform my life.

I don't know exactly why this prayer has become mine. I don't know where it is leading me. It's a mystery, but the mystery is good.

Life, after all, is a mystery—more enjoyable than the best mystery novel, more profound than any I know. Often, its clues come to us in the quietest, most private times of prayer and personal reflection.

Open up. Let them in.

CHAPTER NINE

Put Discipline on Your Side

Nothing significant has ever been accomplished without discipline. In fact, an effective life generally requires what an army general once called "tons of discipline."

And while the word "discipline" may conjure up negative images for some members of my generation, especially—such as being "disciplined" in school for bad behavior or forcing yourself to do something you dislike —the truth is, "discipline" isn't really about that. In fact, it is really the happiest of words.

Discipline simply means doing important things regularly, every day. It means allowing yourself the freedom and forgiveness to reach your loftiest goals in comfortable daily portions, rather than in great exertions. It means staying with and doing what you need to do to accomplish a desired end.

Over time, life's disciplines yield us the richest of all rewards—a life that stands out as accomplished, spiritual, rewarding, and satisfying.

The only difficult aspect of discipline is deciding where and how to make the best use of its power to transform your life. Regular discipline in negative things, we know, only compounds the negative results. But regular discipline in positive things leads to excellence on every level.

Let's take a close look at where and how to put discipline's life-transforming power to work in your life. Be ready for some changes because the results will be remarkable.

Live in the Present

How good are you at living in the moment?

How good are you at being present in the now, really being alive and taking in what is happening right now?

Most of us, after all, don't do very well in this regard. We're distracted, preoccupied, unable to focus.

I've noticed, in my readings, that poets often are our best psychologists. One of the more insightful poets of all time, I think, is Rainer Maria Rilke. And Rilke said this:

> *One lives badly because one comes into the present unfinished, unable, distracted.*

Not long ago, I was meeting with the leaders of Marble Connection, the young singles' group at our church. Because the following Sunday's sermon was about living in the present, a young man who was there said, "Arthur, do you mind if I send something to you?"

I said, "Please do."

He faxed me this poem, by an anonymous writer:

> *First I was dying to finish high school and start college.*
> *And then I was dying to finish college and start working.*
> *And then I was dying to marry and to have children.*
> *And then I was dying for my children to grow old enough*
>   *for school so I could return to work.*
> *And then I was dying to retire.*
> *And now, I am dying . . . and suddenly I realize that I*
>   *forgot to live.*

That's the story of many of our lives.

We can solve that problem.

It's a question of how we organize our minds, how we manage our days, how we regulate ourselves through an hour of time, what we do with the precious gift of time that has been given to us.

Look around you. See the sky. Breathe the air. Feel the world around you. Love the people who share your journey, moment by moment and hour by hour.

Life is *now*.

Follow Your Passion

"In my heart of hearts, I always wanted to be a singer," an acquaintance wrote me. "But I never pursued it. I was afraid I would fail."

We're often afraid of passion. Passion makes us vulnerable, and we can falter. So often, when we put our hearts on the line and try to pursue our life's greatest desires, we get badly hurt.

But what is the alternative? When we close up to protect ourselves—when we fail to strive toward our dreams—we lose what is most childlike and vital about ourselves, and we lose a precious link to the spirit.

Part of the reason people don't pursue their dreams passionately is that they have fallen victim to illusions.

A young pianist believes that success can only be playing concertos with major, important orchestras. Since the chances of doing that are so slim, she finally casts her dream aside—neglecting the fact that there are many other ways to live a life that is full of music. She is thinking in absolutist terms—"All or nothing!" And as a result, she has committed herself to an unrewarding life.

A man loves to work with his hands—he's a natural-born mechanic and has the knack of taking things apart and putting them back together. Yet some time in high school, he decides to cast all that aside—"I'll never make enough money working with my hands!" So he goes off to college, becomes an accountant, and never is really satisfied in his work. He had succumbed to a self-crippling illusion that told him he would have to do something he didn't enjoy in order to make a living. He might have started a technically oriented business, become an engineer, or entered some other field he might have truly enjoyed. Instead, he shut a door to his own best future.

Whatever gift you have been given, whatever dream you've had since you were a boy or girl, you owe a debt to that dream. Let it happen.

You might not become famous or respected or the talk of the town because of what you have done to follow your dream. But you just might—and this is even more important—find a way to reconnect with something childlike and good in yourself. Even if you are just singing in a choir or teaching a few youngsters how to sing—or starting a car-restoration club with some friends, if you are like my mechanically oriented friend—you will be living your dream and making it part of your life.

Yes, you might feel that you are pursuing your dream in a less-than-ideal way. Passion is always a two-sided coin. On one side is joy, and on the other is pain. Yet were you ever passionate about anything that didn't involve pain?

Go into an art museum or gallery and look at a great painting. The artist created it with passion and love and talent, and he or she also struggled at the work to make everything come into place and express emotion.

When writers talk about the process of writing, they often talk about the pain and discouragement as much as the fulfillment and joy.

You owe both to yourself, the pleasure and the frustration, too. Without them, you will not be stretching and growing—or living a life that is right for you.

Give it everything you've got.

Find a Spiritual Community

Jane Kenyon, one of the contemporary American poets profiled by Bill Moyers in his book *The Language of Life,* battled depression until late in her life, without any kind of spiritual or religious support.

She told Moyers that as a little girl she had gone to church with her family but that when she was twelve, she announced that she was too sophisticated for church and she wasn't going to go any more.

And she didn't. Many years later, when she and her husband moved back to his hometown in New Hampshire, she started going to church again, but only because it was the expected thing to do in that community. But something else was going on, too. It wasn't long until she realized that she had an enormous spiritual hunger—something that had been working on her for years without her being aware of it.

She had always been afraid of God, but her new minister talked about a God who overwhelms us with love, a God that was not a God of rules and prohibitions. The minister helped Jane to understand that no matter how bad things get and how deep into the well we fall, life can be forgiving.

Jane Kenyon had been victimized by what religious institutions often do to people. They present faiths as rules and prohibitions. The great religions are not about rules; they are about faith and victory, potential and possibility. Jane was lucky enough to find a minister who took seriously his faith's message of unconditional love. When the struggle with depression became too strong for Jane, her new spiritual understanding saved her life.

"My belief in God, such as it is . . . kept me from harming myself," she recalled. "When I really didn't want to be conscious, didn't want to be awake or aware, I thought to myself 'If you injure yourself, you are injuring the body of Christ. And Christ has been injured enough.'"

Taking part in the right kind of spiritual community—a caring, kind one—is a discipline that can put a kind of "floor" beneath our despair and negativism. We can fall into despair; of course, we all can. Yet with the discipline of membership in the right kind of community, with the right kind of people, there is a lower limit. Those people will catch us and hold us and keep us from falling too far.

I caution you to be careful of religious "authorities" who are about exclusion and breaking rules and falling short.

Seek a forgiving, loving, inclusive place instead. They are out there, for only the price of a little seeking and asking. And they will welcome you.

Live as an Angel

I know of a woman who, like so many of us, has had great turbulence in her life—business problems, a marriage that fell apart, even life-threatening illnesses. She feels she is on a pilgrimage, and every time something challenging happens in her life, she has schooled herself to think, "Now I can move a little further ahead in my life."

"In life, everything doesn't always work out the way we want. But things do indeed work out for the best when you trust that the best is always happening for you."

She told about something that had happened to her a number of years earlier.

"One day in a card store, on impulse, I bought some little coaster-size signs with smiling faces and 'God loves you' written on them. Later, I was walking down the street, and I noticed the car of a man I knew. I reached through the open window and put one of those smiling faces on his car seat. Then I went on my way and really didn't think anything else about it.

"Not too long after that, I was at a meeting with the same man, and he told a story of how overwhelmed with depression he had been one day. He said, 'I went back to my car, and on the seat was one of these little round things with a smile, and the words, *Smile, God loves you*. Being suddenly reminded that God's love was still there for me lifted me up. It might have even saved me from killing myself.'"

"Did you tell him you had done it?" I asked.

"Oh, no, I never did. I believe an angel spoke to me and suggested a way in which I might save that man's life. It was the angel that saved him, not me."

A little kindness is like that—even the smallest gesture can have an impact that is far out of proportion to what we have done.

When we go through life, sowing little seeds of kindness, we act as a positive force in the world.

We can be an angel's agent every day. We can live that way, if we choose. And we can all start in many little ways, today.

Embrace Ecstasy

Another of the poets interviewed by Bill Moyers on his PBS series was Coleman Barks. At one point, Moyers and Barks were talking about those unexpected and wondrous moments in life when we suddenly feel in touch with the eternal—times when the veil of ordinary life seems torn aside and something mystical happens.

We can't plan or demand those encounters with eternity. They just happen. It's the work of the spirit, the activity of God. Yet with the right kind of mindset, we can remain open to those moments every day. And when we are open, we often find that those transcendent moments have a way of happening far more often. Barks spoke of his belief that people have a core that is ecstatic, recognizes these moments, and responds with wonder.

In response to a question from Moyers about what he meant by "ecstasy," Barks began to talk about his boyhood in Chattanooga, Tennessee, and the golden April sunsets he used to see there. When he was a boy, he would get so excited by their beauty that he couldn't stand it. He would lie down and hug himself.

"Mama, Mama, I have that full feeling again," he would say. And she would respond, "I know you do, honey."

Barks felt his mother had given him a great gift: "I grew up knowing it was okay to lie on the floor and hug myself."

I'd like to make a further recommendation. It's not only permissible to hug yourself. It is also permissible to hug *life*.

It is also a very good idea for us to hug each other. We often need to say, "I love you."

We need to say, "I believe in you."

We need to say, "You hurt me, but I forgive you; let's start over again, let's have a resurrection of our relationship."

These things can happen with faith and patience and some hard work. But it all starts by embracing the ecstasy—the ecstasy of life—and welcoming it into your every day.

Lean on Someone Else's Faith

One of my greatest friends, and a great force in my church, was a woman named Clara Macon. She was a wisp of a woman. I don't think she was five feet tall. She was born in the deep South at the turn of the century, and I don't think she had more than an eighth-grade education. She might not have had even as much as that. And if I were asked to describe what her life was like, I would use one word—uphill.

It was as if she kept the waterfall of her life running for nearly ninety years by climbing up a hill with a bucket in hand, scrambling up with one pail full of water at a time.

One day, I realized that I was using my own private name for her. In my mind, I wasn't calling her Clara any more. I'd given her the name "Faith."

If you had to pick a new name for yourself, what would your name be? What is the dominant energy that is coming out of you right now, and has been for a while? What kind of emotion is moving you into the next five minutes of your life?

Faith motivated Clara. She was very loyal to her church. Rarely missed a Sunday. She was an usher. And she didn't want to usher in the sanctuary, where it might have been more prestigious. She wanted to be in the overflow room because she believed that the people who couldn't get into the sanctuary deserved special attention. And week after week after week, she would be there, handing them the bulletin with a smile and energy of faith, giving special attention.

Clara was Faith. And she never knew how many times, when my faith was wavering or weak, I would think "Lean on Clara," and I would get strength from her faith.

This, for me, is a great secret of carrying on through tough times in life. When you don't have the strength and endurance to move ahead and get through, you can lean on someone else, as I leaned on Clara.

Another secret I'd like to share is that I do this quite a bit—with many friends and parishioners and colleagues who don't even know I am "leaning on them" at any given time.

When you feel weak and uncertain and wavering in your faith, make other people's faith part of your own daily outlook and discipline.

Look to someone who is calm, assured, unwavering in his or her orientation toward the positive and the spiritual.

Faith is catching, and other people can sustain you— sometimes, without even being aware that they are doing so.

Replace the "False Idols"

Years ago I was at a banquet. Sitting next to me was the senior vice president of a major international bank. He impressed me. There was a depth to the man. I asked, "Are you active in your church or synagogue?" And he replied, "The rabbi is my best friend."

He talked for a while about his active spiritual life and then said, "I haven't always been this way. For most of my life I lived purely on intellect and didn't believe in all that religious stuff. Then, recently I began to reevaluate my life. I thought of who my heroes were—Abraham Lincoln, Mahatma Ghandi— and two of my old college professors at Cornell.

"All those people were deeply spiritual. They had faith. I began to realize that I was being arrogant. Who was I to think that I could go it alone, when all my heroes were dependent on a higher power?"

So he got back to his religious roots and began a brand new life.

And this man is not alone. A recent Harris poll and stories in major magazines all indicate that something remarkable is happening in America.

It's like a crocus coming up in January. Winter is still around, but there is some life, some beauty coming up in the flowers. There is a spiritual movement where people of all levels of life are beginning to nurture their spirit. It's as if they are saying, "What we're doing isn't working. Something is missing. Our lives are falling apart, the community is not doing very well. We've got to find something else somewhere."

They aren't all going into churches or other houses of worship, but they are beginning to ask spiritual questions.

It's understandable. We are a country of manias—substitute gods, or false idols, if you will.

For instance, we have a mania for gambling. Several years ago, I saw a statistic that documented the fact that 100 million Americans—40 percent of our population—visit gambling casinos every year. And almost every state in the country sponsors lotteries to raise money for the very schools where we teach our children that nothing comes without effort.

Another mania is greed. As long as you can manage to get something that captivates you, and nobody stops you, why not go for it? Something is very wrong with that kind of self-serving thirst for material things.

And we have a mania for violence. We are in love with violence. I despise violent movies. Several years ago, after Bill Cosby's son was killed by a gun, that great entertainer came out and said, "Violence is not entertainment. We must not come to see it as such." Why haven't we heeded his words?

Every time I talk about gun control, people protest, "Arthur, you're getting political." I am not getting political. Gun control is a spiritual, not a political, matter. Violence destroys. Jesus, Ghandi, and Martin Luther King, Jr., all lived nonviolently. They knew that violence doesn't work. We could live according to their example. Yet instead, we have a mania for violence.

We also have an obsession with sex. We have made gods and goddesses of those who promote the pleasure principle of sex. Sex is one of the more beautiful things that God has given to us, but we take it to the lowest level. We find it most alluring when it is denuded of love and responsibility.

However, I think we have finally reached the limit. We've discovered that none of the false idols satisfies our basic need to be fulfilled and happy.

We have finally begun to ask, "What else is there?" We have begun to look to something higher, something better.

We can substitute something true for those false Gods. We can take the low road, or walk higher, in search of something truer, higher, better.

Each of us, no matter where we find ourselves today, can take a spiritual path. Each of us can change direction and feel the weight of negative forces begin to fall away. Freedom!

Again, a simple choice—but beyond all others in its power to free and elate.

Learn to Sacrifice

Not long ago I asked someone, "What do you think of when someone mentions 'sacrifice?'" And the reply was, "Having to do the things I don't want to do."

Like discipline, sacrifice has come to be seen as a negative in our society. *Sacrifice* has come to mean "something to be endured in order to get a reward."

Here are some instances:

Recently a woman I know, speaking with great bitterness, told me her marriage had just ended. She went on and on about how much she had done for her husband. "I gave him the best years of my life. I sacrificed everything for him," she said, "and now look what has happened to me."

How many parents, when disappointed with a child, say, "Look how much I sacrificed for you, and look what you're doing in return."

And how many of us, as employees, having given the very best we had to a company without getting a return in kind, have said, "I sacrificed everything. I'll never do that again in any other job."

The fact is, this is not what sacrifice is all about.

The word *sacrifice* is one of the most beautiful words in our language. It comes from the Latin word *sacrificium*, which means "to make sacred, to make holy."

When we sacrifice, we are being uplifted. We are doing something not only honorable, but divine. A person who sacrifices is making something sacred—bringing holiness into the realm of human action and activity.

Of all the people who have lived lives of self-sacrifice, one of the most remarkable was Mother Teresa. She and the Sisters of Charity are fully present for those who are down and out—the dying, the castoffs, society's lost people.

Mother Teresa, like any of us, could have chosen another kind of life. Yet I never heard her voicing any regret. I never heard her quoted as saying, "Why did I give up everything for the poor? I could have had a nice easy life."

She, through her life, demonstrated that sacrifice creates something sacred. People who sacrifice are performing a holy act.

When we live our lives with the overriding thought, "What's in it for me?" we drain the holiness from life. Life becomes flat, and the more we grasp for pleasure or power, the flatter our lives become. It is a vicious cycle, and the only way we can break out of it is to start living for others with no thought of reward. When we practice this sacrament of giving, our lives can become transcendent.

Are you giving to others? Are you sharing your wealth, energies, and expertise with people whose lives you might transform?

How are you doing? What is your attitude toward sacrifice? Are you living for yourself only, or are you happily working for others? Are you a taker, or are you a giver?

Do you ever think what people will say about you after you die? Years ago, I heard a prayer that goes like this:

> *Dear Lord, help me to live so that, when I die, even the undertaker will be sorry.*

A humorous prayer, to be sure. Yet it contains a thread of truth.

To really make a difference with your life, you must make a difference in the lives of other people. In other words, you must sacrifice.

It's a simple choice that can determine whether your life will be easy and comfortable —or challenging and extraordinary.

Simplify Your Life

"I want to simplify my life."

How many of us have said those very words? Most of us would do well to work at uncomplicating, throwing things out, discarding parts of us that need to be discarded.

How much clutter do you have in your life? How many attachments that are unhealthy? How many addictions that draw you away from what you know you should be doing? How many involvements that are destructive? How much "extra stuff" you don't really need—but cling to nonetheless?

Think of the last time you cleaned out a closet or a chest of drawers. It was probably a long, hard job, but when you finished, you felt light. You felt free.

It's the same with the involvements, the attachments, the addictions of life. It's hard work, but what a difference it makes when, one by one, we shed them.

Pruning seems a fit analogy for simplifying our lives. Gardeners know the importance of pruning. It might look as if they are hurting the plant when they cut branches away. But afterward, the plant grows back fuller and stronger. They have *uncomplicated* the plant—lightened it—and it prospers because of it.

I have my own battles keeping my life simple. In my work room, around the reclining chair where I do my work, I often have stacks of papers and notes. I put things on one little table here, another little table there—and then I've got that wonderful floor where everything else goes.

Everything piles up.

In those stacks are important things and unimportant things, all mixed up. On the occasions when I clean up, I throw away quite a bit. As I reduce the clutter I am constantly choosing what is important to me and what isn't.

In the same way, you can make decisions about what is important to you and what isn't. That kind of thinking can become part of the way you approach each day.

A cluttered life can obscure our deepest desires and needs.

In the twelve-step programs, one of the very practical suggestions is "Live one day at a time." One day at a time! How many of us are distracted by living in the past or in the future?

If living one day at a time is too hard right now, deal with one *hour* at a time. And if that's too much, deal with each five-minute segment. With that intense focus, wonderful things will begin to happen.

Make Choices

The great tenor Luciano Pavarotti tells a story about his father, who was a baker in Modena, Italy. When his father saw how Luciano loved to sing and how beautiful his voice was, he encouraged his son to take voice lessons. But as a young man, Luciano also wanted to go to teachers' college, which is what he did.

After graduating, Luciano asked his father to help him decide what to do with his life. His father gave him this advice: "Luciano, if you try to sit on two chairs, you're going to fall between them. Always choose just one chair to sit on."

As we all know, Pavarotti chose a career in music. There were seven years of pain and frustration and disappointment before he made his professional debut. It was another seven years before he made his debut at the Metropolitan Opera as Rodolfo in *La Bohème*.

Pavarotti always said his father's advice was the most important lesson of his life. Whether you are a bricklayer, an artisan, a businessman—whatever interests you —commit to it. Your focus will bring growth.

Choose one focus. Then bring all your enthusiasm and passion to what you have chosen. Put your whole self into your life. Maintain your passion, no matter what. When life tests you, when life beats you up, hold on. Never let go of your passion.

Welcome Life's Challenges

 The prophet Isaiah had a wonderfully profound mind, and a marvelously poetic way of saying things. In Isaiah 48, verse 10, he says:

Behold, I have refined you, but not like silver; I have tested you in the furnace of adversity.

What a beautifully graphic picture. Aren't we all tested in the furnace, in the heat and the intensity of adversity? In that process, we are refined. We're making something of ourselves.

Many people have read and profited from Scott Peck's books, *The Road Less Traveled* and *Further Along the Road Less Traveled.* Here is what he says about pain:

The quickest way to change your attitude toward pain is to accept the fact that everything that happens to you has been designed for spiritual growth.

That's quite a statement—that pain is designed to further spiritual growth. Scott Peck is reminding us that we are not bodies that happen to have souls; we are souls who happen to have bodies. We are here on this earth in mortal life with a physical body, with material things to deal with, so that we can grow and develop. And pain is a big part of it.

I have a few stories that have helped me in my own life. They seem to me to embody truths that I believe are very important. One of my favorites concerns a laboratory experiment by the English botanist Alfred Russell Wallace, a contemporary of Charles Darwin. Interestingly, he developed the theory of evolution at about the same time that Darwin did. Wallace was ready to publish it when he learned that Darwin had started the experimentation about six months before he had. Wallace, a gentleman, deferred to Darwin, and it is Darwin whom posterity credits with the theory of evolution.

In the experiment, Wallace was in his laboratory observing an Emperor butterfly trying to get free from its cocoon. The struggle was intense, with life-or-death consequences. He wondered, "What would happen if I assisted this process?" So with a knife he made a slit down the length of the cocoon. This is what happened, in his words: "The butterfly emerged, spread its wings, drooped perceptibly and died."

The pain and intensity of the struggle had been denied it, and it had failed to grow. It could not emerge into the world with the strength it needed to survive.

Of course, we don't always welcome adversity with open arms. We don't always welcome pain or setbacks. Yet with the right kind of thinking, we can keep them in perspective and see them as opportunities to grow, strengthen, and excel in our lives. With the right outlook and attitude, we can triumph over adversity.

Seek Peace Every Day

Don't we all long for peace?

We yearn for peace in our own lives—quiet and escape from the ringing phones, the unhappy people, the honking horns that pursue us even into the quiet "private sanctums" of our homes.

Yet that peace seems to elude us.

Similarly, we yearn for peace in the world. We read the morning paper or watch the evening news and are deeply troubled by the events. Why is there still war in the world? Why, at this late point in history, do people still treat others so cruelly and unfairly?

Answers are not easy to find to these deeply disturbing questions. Yet I do know that peace can be found—a deep, abiding peace in your heart that can radiate out to the outside world, affecting other people in positive ways.

And peace can be found, even amid turmoil.

I recall one afternoon several years ago. It was late August, and my wife and I were enjoying the kind of day we like the most on our summer vacations. We worked in the morning, using the phone and the fax machine. Then, with business left behind, we got into our boat about noon and headed to a favorite cove to anchor, have lunch, and read through the afternoon.

That particular day there was a light cloud cover that came over the sun, so I said to my wife, "Lea, let's go on back." So we got ready and pulled anchor and started our quick twenty-minute sail back to the island where we were staying.

In the far distance, we could see a very dark cloud. But it was way, way off. After all, we were accustomed to seeing a few dark clouds during our afternoon sails, and we had learned to pay them little mind. But this time we were in a channel, where the open sea was at our stern and the islands and the mainland ahead of us. Suddenly, the wind came like nothing I had ever seen before. In a second's time, we were being whipped around.

"Lea, I'm going over to that cove," I said.

"Aren't you going to ask my permission?" she asked.

"This is no time to be funny!" I answered.

By the time we were in the cove, visibility was at zero, we couldn't see a thing. The water was coming in sheets at a horizontal angle. I didn't know where I was, what I was doing, what was going on. I knew three things could happen. One, we could crash up against the rocks. Two, we might smash against some boats that were moored in the cove. Or three, we could capsize.

Strange, what goes on in somebody's mind at a time like that. I thought, "Well, I'm supposed to pray or ask God for help." I didn't. But I remembered a letter that I had received years before, from a member of my church who had once landed her plane in very dangerous circumstances. She wrote, "When you're landing a plane and you're in trouble, you don't have time to pray." I really didn't!

The moment finally came when Lea said, "I see a buoy! I see a buoy!"

I recognized the buoy, and I knew where we were. So I did my best to circle it, and stay within sight of it. I was also aware that the storm would probably pass over quickly. And then, in fifteen minutes, it was gone.

Only twenty minutes earlier, we were worried about getting a little bit wet. Now, we were soaked, but elated to be alive! Perspectives change quickly.

Despite the storm that had rocked us, we found peace.

This memory reminds me of the famous story of Jesus. In this story, Jesus and his disciples got into a boat. As soon as they were underway, Jesus put his head down on a pillow and went to sleep. Moments after, there was a storm that came up suddenly and upset everything. The boat was being tossed around. Water was coming over the sides, and the disciples were scared for their lives.

They woke Jesus and said, "Do something!"

In that moment, Jesus did something significant. He decided not to let that storm get inside him. He made a conscious effort to be calm, in control of himself. Then, as the story goes, he said, "Peace! Be still!"

Those words, I believe, were not directed at the storm as much as at the disciples themselves. And everything became calm.

I am reminded of two quotes from Scripture that represent this same process at work:

In quietness and in trust you will find your strength.
(Isaiah, Chapter 30, Verse 15)

Be still and know that I am God.
(Psalm 46, Verse 10)

I can guarantee that each of us—both you and I—will have our lives buffeted by storms in the coming weeks, months, and years.

When that happens, I urge you to remember the words, "Peace! Be still!"

I guarantee that storms will happen because that's the nature of life. But by drawing peace into yourself, every day, you will prevail.

Be Peaceful with Someone Else

We are often tense and compulsive in our lives. And interestingly, those traits usually surface not when we are alone but in our interactions with other people.

In my case, I can be quite compulsive about being on time. I can justify it by saying I want to honor a commitment I've made to someone else by arriving on time. But for me, it really has to do with my need to have a structure and a dependable environment.

My wife and I happen to have very different ideas about time. In fact, my wife probably has a much better time than I do, because when she is concentrating on something, she's really into it—and she stays so.

She doesn't worry about how much time has passed or where she needs to be.

Several years ago while we were on vacation, we were about to attend church, and I said, "Lea, I'd really like to be on time at church today, I don't like to be late."

She agreed. But then, five minutes before it was time to leave, I checked to see if she was ready and was less than happy to see that she was just starting to fix her hair. I said something somewhat critical and went downstairs to fret. To my surprise, however, she appeared in five minutes, looking beautiful. We left for church and arrived on time.

After the service, while we were in a restaurant having brunch, I said, "Thanks for making it on time. I really appreciate it. But tell me, how did you do it?"

Smiling, she lifted her hat a bit—revealing a head still filled with curlers.

She had relaxed, gotten into the flow, and improvised. I, on the other hand, had tightened up and fretted.

She had brought just a little bit of peace to that day in a way I hadn't expected. And since that day, I've tried to follow her lead and think, "Isn't this friction being caused by me as much as the other person? Can't I take the lead in resolving it?"

The answer, inevitably, has been that I can take the initiative in making relationships a little calmer, more peaceful, and more loving. With the right mindset—questioning your own perspective before you criticize, perhaps—you can, too.

Stop Catastrophizing

"Catastrophizing" is a natural human tendency—and it is counterproductive to finding a sense of inner peace.

When we catastrophize, we see the worst possible meaning in any situation, or predict the worst possible outcome.

We're driving down the street, perhaps, when a warning light appears on the dashboard, and we think, "That's it, I'll be stranded here for hours." Or we look back at some minor setback and say, "I'll never recover from that loss."

Perspective is the tool that helps us get past seeing only catastrophic outcomes in life—and invites peace back into our lives.

A number of years ago I befriended a great soul, whose temperament was a great example of perspective.

He was the late Pete McCulley, a journeyman coach in professional football. When in New York, he was a coach with the New York Jets.

Pete—a man of great faith and energy—was always upbeat. Once, when the Jets were having a bad year, I called him after a disappointing loss. I wanted to commiserate. But Pete was not downhearted.

"You know, Arthur," he said, "there were nine hundred million people in China who didn't even know we played! How about that!"

Now, that's perspective. Pete was in the flow—a kind of flow that tells us our problems are small in comparison to those of the rest of the world. And, despite a life of ups and downs, that man always had a deep, abiding sense of faith and inner calm.

Calm and peace don't come from without, but from within. Nobody gives us a better, calmer life—it is ours to claim. Putting our own needs, desires, and problems in perspective—in their place in the "larger scheme of things"—is one key to living a happier life.

Surrender Your Problems
to a Higher Power

The twelve-step recovery process adopted by Alcoholics Anonymous and other organizations leads people on a journey from going it alone, and failing badly, to letting go and letting a higher power help them with their problems and addictions.

The first step is acknowledging you have a problem over which you are powerless—that the problem has helped make your life unmanageable. The second step is believing there is a higher power that can return you to wholeness. The third step is turning your will and your life over to that higher power.

It works. In some people's terminology, it is "letting go and letting God." To others, it means getting into the flow and letting some higher force take control of your problems and recovery.

Most of us remember Roy Campanella. Certainly, many people in New York do! He was a catcher with the old Brooklyn Dodgers, and he is now in the Hall of Fame. One of the first African-Americans to play major-league baseball, Roy was on the same team as Jackie Robinson and was as beloved and valuable.

In the midst of his career, Roy was in an automobile accident which left him a quadriplegic. Most of his rehabilitation work was done at the famous Rusk Institute for Rehabilitative Medicine in New York.

Often, as he wheeled through the corridors of the Rusk Institute, Roy reported, he would stop by a plaque that was mounted on the wall. It contains the words of a poem called "A Creed for Those Who Have Suffered," written by an unknown Confederate soldier:

> *I asked God for strength, that I might achieve.*
> *I was made weak, that I might learn humbly to obey . . .*
> *I asked for health, that I might do great things.*
> *I was given infirmity, that I might do better things . . .*
> *I asked for riches, that I might be happy.*
> *I was given poverty, that I might be wise . . .*
> *I asked for power, that I might have the praise of men.*
> *I was given weakness, that I might feel the need of God . . .*
> *I asked for all things, that I might enjoy life.*
> *I was given life, that I might enjoy all things . . .*
> *I got nothing I asked for—but everything I had hoped for.*
> *Almost despite myself, my unspoken prayers were answered.*
> *I am, among men, most rightly blessed!*

Who, among us, is not so richly blessed—with adversity, yet an abundant life of peace and happiness?

See Angels

When I was a senior at Union Theological Seminary in New York, my father, a Methodist minister, was invited to preach at one of our chapel services. It was a big honor for him. He had always felt somewhat inferior because he had immigrated to this country, and he still spoke with a heavy Italian accent. So for him to preach at such a prestigious seminary in the presence of people like Reinhold Niebuhr and other greats made him very happy and proud.

In his sermon, my father spoke about a man who had an experience with an angel. The story was very real and meaningful for my father. But, sitting in the congregation, I was very embarrassed. In the haughtiness of my youth, I was hardheaded. I duly subscribed to science and the scientific method which tells us, "If you can't see it or prove it in some empirical way, it doesn't exist."

I was allowing that attitude to block me to one of the most important dimensions of spiritual reality.

After the service, I said, "Daddy, why did you have to tell that story?"

"Why, Arthur, what's wrong?" he asked.

"Well, Dad, it doesn't make sense. It isn't realistic," I said.

The conversation ended, but I could sense how deeply I had hurt him. All these years later, I still feel guilty.

When I was twenty-three, I was too sophisticated to pay much attention to the phenomenon of angels. I believed that angels were the creation of the vivid, dramatic imagination of people in Biblical times. I believed that those people had needed to create the notion of angels to help them understand life's more puzzling mysteries.

If I believed in angels at all, I relegated them to a particular time in history, when people were much simpler than they are today. God provided angels because people needed them and would only respond to messages borne by heavenly beings.

Today, I'm in a different place. I believe in angels. I've come a long way in my understanding.

I believe we are surrounded, as we are surrounded by the air that we breathe, by a higher level, another dimension, a place of the spirit. That spiritual place, with all of its dynamism, is where we can greet messengers who give us insights into a more spiritual realm.

You can call angels by any name you wish. But the important thing is, stay attuned. Because something does surround you—protecting you, bringing good news, lightening your heart. You don't have to earn this benefit; you only have to accept it. It's there, waiting for you.

Make that kind of thinking part of your discipline and perspective on the world. And be ready for remarkable results.

CHAPTER TEN

Heed the Call to Leadership

There is a major misconception about leadership.

Leadership is not an ego thing. Leadership is about giving.

Wherever you are in your life, you can be a leader. You become one by serving others. It is just as simple—and just as difficult—as those words imply.

Because true leadership has nothing to do with seeking advancement or personal rewards. It is all about helping other people—reaching out and caring and helping and loving as much as your capabilities allow.

You can lead in your life, starting today, from exactly where you are. Leadership is a call you can obey. In this chapter, we'll begin to find out how.

You *Can Lead*

 Consider, first, what makes a leader? If you ask yourself that question, you may find that a number of images and answers come to mind:

- *A leader stands tall.*
- *A leader speaks commandingly.*
- *A leader is able to make tough decisions.*
- *A leader has personal magnetism.*

That question "What makes a leader?" may even cause your mind to conjure up the image of someone famous—a politician, successful CEO, general, athletic coach, or historical figure.

Those are all valid images of leadership. After all, good leaders often do stand straight and tall. Often, they are good public speakers. Sometimes, they achieve fame and wealth.

Yet I think that to dwell on those visible traits of leadership can be misleading.

You can be a leader in your life even if you don't possess many of those traits—or even any of them. You can be a leader whether you are the CEO of a company or the receptionist.

You can lead in your life, starting today, from exactly where you are.

To become a leader, the internal traits are what really count. Leadership is a call you can obey.

Start Leading Today

"I'm not ready to be a leader," my friend Diane says. "Who am I? Just an executive like many others. Talk to me about leadership when I'm running a company. I'm not ready for it now."

Diane is modest. Yet she is thinking about leadership in the wrong way. You can lead with your life starting today. And you can start right where you are.

I think that few of us would deny the fact the people I'm about to describe are true leaders, even though they aren't CEOs, athletic coaches, or political figures. They might not all fit our preconceived criteria of what leaders are supposed to be, yet they are leaders nonetheless:

- *The community leader in inner-city Chicago who started a home for unwed mothers and helped many of them rebuild their lives.*

- *The Hasidic man from Crown Heights, Brooklyn, who works an anonymous job in a store from Monday through Friday, but who is revered in his community as an insightful scholar and gifted teacher of the young in his Yeshiva.*

- *The elderly invalid who, although infirm and confined to a wheelchair, has started a concert series and a book-discussion group in the convalescent home where he resides. He is adored by all—a true trendsetter.*

The ninety-year-old great-grandmother who never attended college or pursued a career—but whose wisdom and devotion to her family have made her an adored family matriarch.

So we see, leadership is not something that can be practiced only by a special group of privileged people.

You can lead from where you are today. We all can.

How? There are many ways. We can take a positive attitude. Set prejudice aside. Listen to people, instead of rushing in to tell them what we believe.

You've read about those steps in earlier chapters of this book. And they all add up to leadership.

In sum total, we might compress all that advice into the simple words, "Take the higher road."

Build Your Life from Your Center

Have you known someone who was always striving, trying to excel, but whose dreams seemed always just beyond reach?

I think we all have known people like that. And, if you will take a moment to think about such people you have known, I suspect that you will come to the same conclusion about them that I have.

In nearly all cases, these people are not operating from their true centers. Haven't you, in fact, known people like these:

Charles wants to be a successful entrepreneur. He's tried several business ventures, but things have yet to "click" for him. Nobody really wants to tell Charles the problem—although he badly needs to hear it. He is simply not cut out to be an entrepreneur. He's a warm, caring person—someone so gentle, he almost seems to invite others to take advantage of him. Charles would be a wonderful teacher, counselor, therapist, or member of the clergy. But he keeps trying to stretch into areas that don't suit him. He's not operating from his real base of power.

Letitia has spent the first ten years of her professional life trying to be a professional singer. Now, Letitia has a remarkable, cultivated voice, and with the right kind of personality, she would stand as good a chance to build a career in classical music as many other singers. Yet, the truth is, she seems ill-equipped to take all the "hard knocks" that come with that profession. Whenever she sings for an audition and doesn't get the job (an experience classical singers must learn to live with frequently), she becomes deeply upset. Also, she suffers acute emotional distress before performances—another clear indication that she may be pursuing the wrong path. Yet she seems resolute in pursuing her intended path until the last possible moment in her life.

Letitia is a remarkable person with many abilities and skills. She loves music and communicates its joy to others. She is immediately loved by children—I've seen it happen many times. With only a little "tinkering," she could find another career path that would tap these abilities and live a much more satisfying life.

She, like Charles, is not operating from her center.

It is easy to see the obstacles that these two capable people have placed in their own paths—and far harder to recognize those that we have placed in our own. How can we discern our "center," and how can we build upon it to lead a more dynamic, richer life? There is no one prescription or success formula.

Your true calling, which emerges from your center, is a growing, evolving combination of hopes, dreams, and abilities. How can you identify it? By considering the following factors in a playful, nonpressured way:

- Your dreams, visions, and ambitions and hopes. Or, in other words, the vision of your future that excites and stimulates you in a positive way.

- Your higher aspirations. In other terms, the kind of mark you would like to leave on the world.

- What other people tell you about you. Ask someone you trust what you should be doing with your life. Ask them what your skills and strengths are. The answers they give may surprise you and lead to new possibilities.

- Your preferred settings and activities. I've known many office workers who would really prefer to be working outdoors. Similarly, I've known people with tremendous personal warmth who get pigeonholed into office jobs where they hardly ever see another human being.

- Where you're evolving. Often, the dreams and ambitions we had in childhood can be enlarged and enriched, based on the experiences we have had in our adult lives. I know one woman, for example, who recovered from cancer and combined that experience with her lifelong love of people to forge a new career working with cancer patients. As we experience more, our goals and missions should change.

What is your center? Of course, I can't tell you in this book. I can only urge you to search, and then search some more. Life is ever-changing and wonderful. Just ask. If you are truly willing to receive answers, life will yield its messages up to you.

Help People in Small Ways

One day I got on an elevator, going down. On the elevator, a woman with a coat over her arm was trying to affix a cufflink to the cuff of her blouse, but she was having trouble. After a moment I said, "Can I help you?"

Now, I was in New York, and I fully expected the woman to say no. But she looked up and said, "Yes, would you? That would be very nice!"

The elevator arrived at the first floor, and we moved over to the side of the lobby. I tried several times, but failed to make progress with the cufflink. Meanwhile, the woman was sharing some small talk, saying, "I can do it with my right hand but not with my left."

"I know," I said. "I have one just like this. I can't do it with my left hand either!"

Well, in a minute or so the cufflink was in place, the woman thanked me, and I went on. It was just a small, friendly point of connection between two people in their busy days.

But the episode made me think about what that woman had really accomplished in that moment. She allowed another human being, stranger though I was, to help her. She could have taken the attitude that communicated "No, I'll do it myself if it kills me!"

It was a small thing, yet two people were helped. She was helped, obviously, but I was helped too. You see, I had the satisfaction of doing something for somebody else. It made me feel good.

An anecdote in Scripture reinforces this same point. In Matthew (Chapter 25:31–46)—one of the most significant passages in the entire Bible, I believe—Jesus tells his disciples the difference between those who will be invited into the heavenly kingdom and those who will not.

Did Jesus talk about believing? About having the right doctrine? No, He didn't mention those things. What He said was, "Remember the time when I was hungry and you gave me food? Thirsty, and you quenched my thirst? A stranger, and you welcomed me? Naked, and you clothed me? Sick, and you cared for me? In prison, and you visited me? When I was in need, and you came and helped me and met my needs?"

His disciples didn't understand the symbolism. They were puzzled and replied, "When did we do anything like that for you?"

But Jesus said, "When you did it for one of the least of the members of the human family, when you did it for anybody, you were doing it for me too."

So when we lovingly reach out with care and meet someone else's needs, we are doing it on behalf of something far, far bigger. With even small gestures, we are doing our part to build a better world.

Excel within Your Abilities

Some of the best advice I ever received came when I was sixteen years old. I was a junior in high school in Portland, Maine, and I was first trombonist in the school band. That year, I saw a notice that announced a music contest I really wanted to enter. The prize would be a free trip to New York City and the Metropolitan Opera.

Well, for a kid from Maine, that was an exciting opportunity, and I decided to enter.

There was a problem, however, and a big one. I was not an especially good musician. In fact, I'd already stopped taking lessons. But I gathered up my courage and told my younger brother's violin teacher what I wanted to do. I asked him to help me prepare.

Mr. Howe, the teacher, told me, "I will help you under the following conditions: First, if you work with me, you will decide you are going to win. Never doubt that fact.

"And second, this is the reason you are going to win: Most of the contestants will choose music that is beyond them. They will want to show off, to double-tongue and triple-tongue and do all kinds of fancy things, and under the pressure of the contest they won't do well. But you are going to select a piece of music that is within your ability—and you are going to master it. And you are going to win."

He meant what he said. Before I even put the trombone to my lips, Mr. Howe sat me down and over a period of time, drilled me on every note of the music. He played it for me. I counted it out, I heard it, I knew what to expect. By the time I picked up my instrument, I had the music in my head, and I knew it.

Then I practiced it all over and over and over. Mr. Howe arranged to have me invited to every possible music program and afternoon tea party in Portland, so I could practice playing my music before an audience.

When the day came for the contest, there were twenty contestants in Portland's Frye Hall. Four of us would win. And Mr. Howe was right: Nearly every other contestant was better than I was, and most of them had chosen something too difficult to play. They faltered, but I played what I had prepared confidently and capably.

I wasn't surprised when the judges announced the winners, and I was one of the four.

That was a lesson that has served me well. Ever since that day, I have sought to follow Mr. Howe's advice, which I sum up in these words:

Operate within your ability, never beyond it. That's where your strength lies. If you do, you can master any challenge life places in your path.

Success is rarely achieved in the grand, great wins. It is the result of many small victories that lie well within our abilities.

Live on Your Truth

Life can become truly wonderful when we are in tune with the best that is in us. In fact, there may be no other way to move the experience of living from the level of satisfactory to sensational.

And, as with other topics we've explored in this book, the choice is up to you.

For many years, I knew a man who seemed to move through life in a state of constant agitation. In all those years, I never saw him calm. I'd frequently hear him put people down, or complain about what a difficult day he was having. Yet as far as I knew, he had no real reason to be upset or agitated. He had been born into considerable wealth. In many ways, he had an easy life. But despite what seemed to be good fortune, he was a man of dissatisfaction and prejudice.

When he was very old and gravely ill, he asked me to visit with him. He was reflecting on his life and wanted to talk about it. I sensed that he was at the point in his life where he was willing to talk openly and frankly. He knew his life was really over.

He told me that when he was very young, he had very great ambitions for his life. He even had one extraordinary, life-transforming event. When he was attending a youth conference, he had a strong message telling him that God wanted him to do something very significant with his life.

He described how excited that revelation made him at the time, and how much good he planned to do with his life. He planned to be a person who would not only be successful, but significant. He wanted to become a person who would lift the lives of others around him, enabling other people to lift themselves from poverty and live better lives.

"That was a wonderful thing to happen when you were young," I said.

A few moments of silence followed, then the man spoke.

"I didn't do any of it," he answered.

And though I tried to reassure him by pointing to the many achievements of his life, I realized that I could not give him back something very important—something it was his job to make part of his life.

There are certain things people have to give themselves. No one else has that ability.

As we were talking, I thought of what Thoreau said—that one of the worst things that can happen to any of us is to come to the end of our lives and discover that we haven't really lived.

My friend, in a sense, had been given a great gift—a vision for his life. Yet he betrayed the best that was in him, and the result had been constant inner agitation. He had never known inner peace.

An important step is this:

Find your truth.

Work to discern whatever inside of you is truly *you*.

There was a reason you were born. Discover it, the purpose for your being.

Our fingerprints are all different. And of the billions and billions of people who have lived in the eons of time, every single person has a different soul imprint.

There is a purpose for every soul brought onto the face of this world. A major challenge for you and every human being is to discover that purpose for being.

Talk to your inner self. Work on it. Ask, "In my heart of hearts, what will leave me fulfilled and accomplished when I am drawing to my close?"

Your heart's desire might be to help people, to live in a way that will inspire your own children to live fuller, deeper lives. It might be to change careers. It might be to write a novel or paint a painting—or simply to love life more each day.

Life is an open book where you can write your own story if you have the courage.

What will you write? What are you writing *now?*

When your whole being is focused around your heart's desire, your calling, your values—your true self—you can achieve inner peace and a life that is truly rich.

Set Resolutions You Can Achieve

It's often said that effective leaders have the ability to set goals and then reach them. That's very, very true. Why do resolutions sometimes fail to work?

One reason is that people have highly unrealistic expectations. For instance, they want to lose weight, and they want to get it over with as quickly as possible. So they resolve to lose fifty pounds in thirty days. They start with high expectations and a lot of determination, and that lasts for about a week because the goal is unattainable. Once they discover they haven't lost enough weight to reach their goal, they become discouraged and give up.

The second reason resolutions fail to work is that people don't take them seriously enough. Resolutions require a commitment. Thinking and talking are cheap; actions cost something.

A third reason resolutions fail to work is that people become impatient with themselves. They might keep a resolution for a few days or weeks, but then they backslide. They become frustrated. They think they have failed totally, when they have only just missed a step for a moment.

Perhaps the biggest reason we fail to reach our goals is that we make too many of them at one time. It is normal to seek a number of areas where we need to change, and to list them all and attack parts of them at the same time. But this method often hinders our ability to attain any one goal completely. It's usually impossible to concentrate on so many things at once.

A final reason resolutions fail is because the word resolution *itself usually has a negative connotation for us.* We feel it means depriving ourselves of something.

But really, *resolution* has a wonderful meaning. It comes from the Latin word *resolvere*, which literally means "to look back and solve the problem." It also means "to set yourself free"—that is, to be free from limitations that have bound you.

That changes the whole character of the word, doesn't it?

So, what kind of thinking stands a better chance of helping you reach your goals?

First of all, why not take just one area, one dimension of yourself, and give your complete attention and all of your energies to that and to nothing else? If you focus on that problem and succeed with your resolution, your success will affect every dimension of your life, and you can take that energy and solve more and more problems with your life.

I recall one man I knew who first lost weight. Then he brought new focus to his career, changed jobs, and moved significantly forward with his ambitions. Then he met a woman—finally, the woman he called his "soul mate"—and took his life to a higher dimension.

When we move ahead in one area of our lives, we prepare the way for progress in all other areas, too. The wisest men and women have always known to start small in reaching their plans. Bigger comes later. The key is to get started now, where and when you can.

Be Your Own Person

 I place before you a remarkable fact: Out of the five billion people now living on the face of the earth, no two human beings are just alike. Every one is different from everyone else. And of the many more billions who have lived since the beginning of time, every individual has been unique.

So in a very real way, that means you are a special edition. Have you ever thought of yourself as a special edition? Special editions are very important.

Once, while touring the Scandinavian countries, I took a free afternoon to shop for a few gifts. Sweden is famous for glass, so I went from one shop to another until finally I found a very pretty vase—deep blue with delicate lines winding around it. It was a lovely piece, so I took it to a salesman and said, "I would like to buy this."

He turned over the piece and showed me that the piece was truly unique. It was a special edition, signed by the craftsperson who had made it with his own hands. Suddenly, it took on a new level of meaning for me. I would never see another vase just like it, no matter how long I lived or where I traveled.

It was unique, just as each person is unique. Each of us is his or her own person.

So, how do we become our own person? Well, there are some steps you need to take, and there are some traps you must avoid.

Let's look at the traps first—traps that cause us to be identified with things that are not *us*.

Possessions—A major trap is to become too closely identified with our possessions, trying to gain prestige from things, such as an automobile. Marketing experts say they can sell us the car that will make us feel that we are a somebody. Another possession we use to identify ourselves is our address: We want to live in the "right" place, which will conjure up the right image in the minds of all people who hear where we live.

But although our possessions might be an expression of who we are, they never truly become who we are. As Confucius once wrote, "A house cannot bring honor to a man (or woman). The man (or woman) must bring honor to the house."

Our jobs—For many of us, all of our identification is connected with our position, our job. I knew one man who had the same job his whole life. When he was twenty years old he went to work as a salesperson for a wholesale grocer, and when he died at the age of ninety-two, he still had some accounts.

A job is an opportunity for us to grow, to express ourselves. That special edition that we are has an opportunity to blossom. But if we become so closely identified with one job and then lose that job or retire, who are we?

Pearl Bailey, the singer, made a pithy remark about people who wear labels. She said, "I hate labels. I never wear labels. Anybody who has to hang something around his neck to say who he is, he isn't."

Envy—A third trap that prevents us from being our own person is trying to be somebody else. Perhaps we have a hero or heroine, some role model, whom we want to emulate. We study that person to see how successful, how well organized, how wonderful he or she may be. Then we say, "I will be just like that person."

That's a mistake. That is imitating. If you truly see yourself as a special edition, you can learn from a role model who has reached a standard of excellence, but you cannot be that person.

What you can be is your own very best self, and if you can develop that attitude, you may well exceed the standard of the people you have admired.

What steps do you need to take to become your own person? Well, in my opinion, there are two things you need to do:

The first is to get in touch with something deep within yourself. It is more than a feeling; it's a deep underlying thirst. It is your "calling." And many jobs can fit into your calling.

There may be some profound thirst that has been with you all your life, letting you know you are called to work with your hands, or with children, or with the infirm, or even outdoors.

There are many ways to fit a life into your calling—and living an authentic life that's based on it will bring you more rewards in life than all the prestigious job titles or possessions.

The second thing you need to do to be your own person is to get in touch with some higher power—something spiritual in your life. I don't believe a person can come into his own unless he is in touch with this spiritual dimension.

A fish out of water is still a fish, but a fish doesn't function unless it is in water. Human beings outside the spiritual realm are still human beings, but they won't come into their own unless they get in touch with a creative, spiritual force.

It's been my experience that taking these two steps gets you started on the road toward being your own person and toward affirming the wonderful fact that you are a special edition. When you are shining that unique beauty that is yours alone, you will take your place among all the other unique people in the wonderful mosaic of humanness and life.

Never Stop Thanking

There are two words in the vocabulary of living that ennoble and ease all human interaction. Without them, the world would be a cold and harsh place. They are *thank you*.

- *Thank you for holding the door for me.*
- *Thank you for the favor.*
- *Thank you for offering to help.*
- *Thank you for being there for me.*
- *Thank you for being my friend.*

Every time the words *thank you* are spoken, at least two people benefit. One is the person who expresses thanks. The other one who benefits is the one thanked. The one who has done the kindness, been the friend, done the favor, held the door—that person needs to hear words of appreciation. We must never take that kindness for granted.

Think about your environment. You are surrounded by people you need. How about approaching some of them and saying "thank you!"?

Have you ever tried thanking the bus driver or subway conductor?

You might say, "Why thank them? They're doing their jobs."

But you do your job, and doesn't it make a difference when somebody says, "Thank you for what you're doing"?

If you go a bit deeper in thinking about your life, there's another group of people who significantly affect who you are.

These are people who have helped you grow, who have walked with you through personal trials, who through the example of their lives have opened up possibilities for you.

Over the years, I've written a couple of dozen letters to people who have had an influence on me. Most of them wrote me back or called me. There was a deeper bonding between us because I have said, "Thank you. You made a difference in my life, and I appreciate it."

But even when there was no response, I benefited from remembering and thanking them. There was a strengthening and enlivening of a sense of interconnectedness, a demonstration of our need one for the other.

I invite you, if you have not done this before, to think about somebody who has enriched your life. Reach out to tell that person how much you've been helped, and say thank you, not with just a phone call but with a letter—something that can be saved and read over and over.

There's a great story in the Bible about recognizing the generous giver. Whenever I read it, I am reminded of all the times I have forgotten to say "thank you." Sometimes I've simply been oblivious, lost in my own thoughts, my own busyness, my own troubles, and I just haven't thought to give thanks. This is the story:

One day Jesus was approached by ten lepers. Because lepers were not supposed to get too close to other people, they stood a distance from Jesus and called, "Have mercy on us."

And Jesus said, "Turn around, go, and show yourselves to your priests."

That was a strange directive. But obviously Jesus projected strength and authority, so they did as he asked. As they were walking, they began to feel strange. They looked at each other and discerned something unusual was happening to them.

They were being healed, coming into wholeness. It was a miracle.

They did as most people would have done. They began to celebrate, running and jumping and cheering and hugging one another. They were wild with happiness.

Then one of the ten stopped for a moment. He began to think about who was responsible for what was happening. So he turned around and went back to find Jesus. He fell to the ground and effusively gave thanks.

Jesus was pleased. Like any of us, he needed to know that when he reached out to help, not only was the help accepted and used but the person he had helped would take a moment to say, "Thank you, I appreciate your help."

But Jesus also noticed that only one of the ten healed lepers had returned. Quietly he asked, "Where are the nine?"

That question always gets to me.

Never, ever must we take for granted what others do for us. We need to educate ourselves continuously in the fine art of saying, "Thank you. Thank you. You've done something very special for me."

Do Good
for No Good Reason

Mark Twain had a unique perspective on doing good. He said, "Always do right. Some people will be gratified, and the others will be astonished."

Doing good—with no expectation of reward—can revolutionize your life. You will be transformed.

Another way to say this is to live so that you bless each moment.

You can bless the moment, bless the situation, bless the problem, bless the challenge. You can even bless your enemy and things that you don't like.

This was a central message in the thinking of Martin Buber, one of the great souls of this century and a Jewish scholar and mystic.

When I was a student at Union Theological Seminary in New York, he used the library there, and he would often eat in the refectory. He was a short, stooped man, and he was very old at the time. And we would say, "There's Martin Buber." But none of us ever went to sit with him. I wish I knew then what I know now about this remarkable man. Today, I would simply sit in his presence and try to absorb the spirit of the man.

His great legacy was a little book called *I and Thou* that puts forth the concept of blessing other people without any expectation of reward.

He encouraged a deep, spiritual transformation in human behavior in which we see others as "thou"— not "it"—and honor them.

He taught that our job in living is to relate to other people as if they were souls to be cherished and deeply, deeply respected.

That's the ultimate in blessing. Never to use anybody. Never to take advantage of anyone. To expect the best from life, and give the best, because we have too much respect for each other's soul to act otherwise.

Put Other People First

It may come as a surprise to many readers of this book, but being at the head of a large religious institution is not terribly different from running a company or business enterprise. It takes a lot of leadership skills, not only from the pulpit or in worship but in performing the day-in, day-out duties of organizing and motivating a group of colleagues.

There are many well-known principles of leadership I've tried out along the way. One is to "lead by example"—which holds that the best way to inspire people to act a certain way is to act that way yourself. If you expect honest communications, communicate honestly. If you expect punctuality, be on time.

Another respected leadership principle is to take risks and be courageous. Another still is to empower people to make decisions on their own.

Those are all wonderful approaches to leading other people, and they work well. But I'd like to tell you about another leadership secret I've discovered.

Put other people first.

Another term for this style of leadership is "Back-Row Leadership." How does it work? You lead other people by *allowing them to lead you.* Wherever you are in your life—whatever your position—here are some ways to get this principle working for you:

- *Take the time to establish a personal bond with each person in your life.* A legendary basketball coach once told me, "The one-on-one, personal time I spend with each member of my team is the greatest motivator there is."

- *Believe in people and what they can do.* I have too often observed that people in authority start from the opposite vantage point. They believe that they are smarter and more capable than anyone else. Real leaders, in contrast, look for the best in people and, as a result, they often get just that.

- *Always remain quiet and listen before you talk.* When a person comes to you with a problem he or she is unable to solve, do not be too quick to offer an opinion or solution. Allow the other person to describe the problems he or she is facing—and to formulate his or her own solutions. More often than not, they will be the right ones.

- *Ask, "Am I the cause of a problem here?"* Often, when you are seen as an authority, other people hold back before telling you you have done something wrong. I recall that a staff member was once unable to complete an assignment I had given him because I had expressed unrealistic expectations for the outcome—the fault was mine, not his. He told me, and set things right on his own. Unless you can get your ego out of the way, that can't happen. You stand little chance of becoming a leader.

- *Let people suggest new ideas and approaches to you.* It's all well and fine to be a leader who comes up with a steady flow of good ideas. Yet how much more productive it can be to be a leader who keeps the doors open so that each person he sees is eager to present new ideas and solutions. Listen, and then listen some more.

- *Provide opportunities for others to shine.* Jane Seiling, author of a book called *The Membership Organization,* reports that, when she was a secretary, she learned that many customers who were calling her company were getting busy signals. She told her boss, the CEO of the company, and her boss gave her the authority to select and purchase a new phone system for the firm. "When I saw that I was empowered to do something, horizons opened up for me," she says. Today, she is a successful author and business consultant. You, like that CEO, can empower others to take authority and excel in their lives—or you can stifle them and shut them down. It's a simple choice you can make.

So the message is, you need goals and a vision and energy and follow-through. But without the foundation of people who feel empowered to excel, your success can only be short-lived.

Open up. Let people lead you. The results can transform you into an inspiration to all those around you.

Pass Grace Along

Any gift we receive—whether a gift of love, of compassion, of forgiveness, of understanding, even a material gift—we can never keep. If we try to keep the gift, if we try to guard it and hold it tight, we become even more likely to lose it. The gift loses its effectiveness; it doesn't have power anymore.

But if we give that gift away, pass it on, that gift keeps flowing and flowing, on and on. Its rewards first benefit other people, then come back to us.

And the opposite is also true. When we have passed along harm, that harm afflicts other people, then has a way of coming back to harm us again.

I once saw this latter principle at work with John, a member of our church staff. As the two of us discussed a church program, he told me, "Arthur, I hope you won't do what you did to me a year ago. You criticized me!"

What was he talking about? I couldn't imagine. I asked when I had criticized him. As he described the incident, I remembered the encounter and recalled there had been no criticism in my heart. I told him he had misunderstood me. I apologized somewhat defensively, and went on to explain myself again.

The next morning during my quiet time, an image of John came into my mind's eye as I recalled the conversation of the preceding day. I felt some voice was telling me: "Arthur, you were very defensive. You injured that person even more with your explanation. Go and apologize today, and ask forgiveness, no strings attached."

Another, counterbalancing voice then answered the first, saying, "Forget it! You already apologized once. And really, you meant something different when you made the comment that triggered the bad feelings in the first place!"

It was the voice of pride, telling me I didn't have to go back to that person again.

But the first voice came through again: "Go and make it a clean slate."

So later that day I apologized to John, with no defensive explanation. It was a very rich moment. I saw his eyes become clearer, heard him telling me, relieved, "I forgive you."

And in that moment I sensed a deeper bonding in our relationship.

Where we have been given a gift—a gift of healing, a gift of compassion, a gift of forgiveness—whatever it is, we don't own it. We can't hold on to it; we have to give it away. And when we do, a remarkable thing happens.

We don't have less love, happiness, or compassion in our hearts. We have so much more.